T0154925

## RAND

# An Exploration of Cyberspace Security R&D Investment Strategies for DARPA

*"The Day After . . . in Cyberspace II"*

Robert H. Anderson, Anthony C. Hearn

**National Defense Research Institute**

Prepared for the
Defense Advanced Research Projects Agency

# Preface

This report describes the results of an exercise sponsored by the Defense Advanced Research Projects Agency (DARPA) using the RAND "The Day After..." methodology to elicit the views of participants on research and development investment strategies addressing the security and safety of systems and networks supporting various U.S. physical and functional infrastructures. The exercise was held on March 23, 1996 in Washington D.C., and involved approximately 60 participants from government, universities, and commercial industries involved with the U.S. information infrastructure.

This report should be of interest to persons interested in defensive information warfare, cyberspace security and safety, and technology R&D initiatives related to information system security.

The research reported here was conducted within the Acquisition and Technology Policy Center of RAND's National Defense Research Institute, a federally funded research and development center (FFRDC) sponsored by the Office of the Secretary of Defense, the Joint Staff, and the defense agencies. It builds on an earlier and ongoing body of research work within that Center on the national security implications of the information revolution.

# Contents

Preface ............................................................................................................ iii

Figures ........................................................................................................... vii

Tables ............................................................................................................. vii

Summary ......................................................................................................... ix

Acknowledgments ......................................................................................... xv

1.  Introduction ............................................................................................ 1
    The Purpose of This Exercise ............................................................... 1
    The Scenario and Methodology Used for This Exercise ................... 2
    The Conduct of the Exercise ................................................................. 5

2.  Findings and Research Suggestions ................................................... 8
    Step 1.  Observations and Findings .................................................... 8
    Step 2.  Observations and Findings .................................................. 12
    R&D Investment Suggestions ............................................................ 13

Concluding Remarks ..................................................................................... 21

Appendix

A.  List of Participants .............................................................................. 23

B.  Scenario and Instructional Materials Used in Exercise ................. 27

References ....................................................................................................... 67

# Figures

1.1. "Classic" Three-Step Day After Exercise Methodology ........................ 2
1.2. Revised Two-Step Day After Exercise Methodology ............................ 3

# Tables

1.1. Cyberspace Incidents Used in Scenario .................................................. 4
1.2. Agenda for Exercise ................................................................................... 6

# Summary

During the past several years, a RAND-developed "The Day After..." exercise methodology has been developed and used to explore strategic planning options, both for nuclear proliferation and counter-proliferation, and, more recently, for questions involving "security in cyberspace" and "information warfare (IW)." On March 23, 1996, a "The Day After...in Cyberspace" exercise with approximately 60 participants was conducted at RAND's Washington D.C. offices, under the sponsorship of the Defense Advanced Research Projects Agency. The purpose was to generate suggestions and options regarding research and development initiatives to enhance the security of the U.S. information infrastructure.

The scenario used in this exercise involved a Mideast crisis situation, with Iran as an aggressor. We used a variation of the scenario that had been used earlier to explore other aspects of planning for cyberspace security, as documented in Molander, Riddile, and Wilson (1996).

Participants in the exercise spent approximately three hours in individual groups, and another two hours in plenary sessions, discussing both short-term technical fixes to counter IW attacks that were hypothesized to occur in the year 2000 and longer-term research strategies that could be initiated now to avoid significant vulnerabilities in the future. These discussions ranged over known problems with the current information infrastructure, and both common wisdom and some novel approaches to tightening the security of those systems on which our nation depends. We highlight below some of the observations and suggestions resulting from these discussions that appear to be relevant to DARPA's planning for R&D investments in the field of cyberspace security.

## Critical Concepts

• *"Safe havens" should be developed as a fallback means for systems when under attack*

It may be possible to configure key infrastructure systems so that they can quickly be isolated into self-sufficient regional systems in a crisis. If, in a matter of seconds or minutes, the energy grids or telecommunication systems could be isolated into smaller units, the resulting smaller units might become safe havens protected from remote attack. At a later safe time, the units might be reassembled into an interconnected system.

• *Tactical warning/attack assessment (TW/AA) is an important concept for cyberspace security*

It was agreed that TW/AA is important, and that there is currently little infrastructure in place to perform these activities. Discussants concluded that there must be a clearinghouse (a "National IW Center"?) to collect, collate, and uncover patterns in cyberspace attacks that span systems in all key infrastructures: transportation, power, finance, communication, defense, and so forth.

## Operational Aspects

• *Operational aspects of security (dealing with people, procedures, regulations) are vitally important to any solution*

There was considerable discussion of "operational" aspects of security that may be less amenable to R&D, but are deemed vitally important to any overall security posture. It was clear that issues related to people, procedures, regulations, training, education, and so on were a critical adjunct to any successful security technology initiative. The following operational aspects were specifically mentioned:

> *The concept of "cyberspace hot pursuit" needs attention.* We need software tools to aid in the backtracing of incidents, to discover the perpetrator.

> *We need procedures for the prepositioning of backup systems and software.* The concept of "safe havens" in information systems was discussed, along with the related idea of prepositioning verifiably accurate software (and possibly hardware) for rebaselining corrupted systems.

> *"Red teams" are needed to test system defenses.* The groups tended to concur that active testing of system defenses is an important means for assessing system

security. Testing should be expanded to cover all key national information infrastructure systems.

*Map the networks.* We need maps of the interconnections among the networks of cyberspace to resolve questions such as: How do energy grid control systems depend on the public switched telephone network (PSTN)? Some agency(ies) should be tasked with maintaining an updated map of the tens of thousands of links and interrelationships and interdependencies among key networks.

*Personal ID verification systems should be employed.* Participants felt it was important to employ such systems on all links into the infrastructure, including access through dial-in maintenance ports.

*The concept of "human firewalls" should be considered in an emergency.* As systems are decomposed into "safe havens" (see above) when an attack is imminent, or during an attack, it might be possible to insert a human as an intelligent verification device to pass judgment before various people and systems are allowed to obtain access to critical nodes and links in the infrastructure.

*A "two-person rule" might be used for critical decisions or system changes.* Just as firing a nuclear missile requires the cooperation of (at least) two individuals, we should consider the advantages (weighed against additional costs and impediments) of requiring two persons to authorize and allow any key change to critical system software, or to implement a decision regarding critical links or nodes.

*Consider better pay and status for critical system operators.* Personnel might then be less vulnerable to bribes, and less likely to become disgruntled or disaffected. It is widely understood that the trusted insider poses the greatest threat to critical information systems.

## U.S. Government Roles

In discussing possible roles for the U.S. government in enhancing cyberspace security, three specific analogies were mentioned:

*Automobile safety regulations.* The U.S. government, in cooperation with the auto industry, created regulations to make automobiles safer. The safety and security of cyberspace is now in a situation analogous to that of the automobile industry many years ago.

*The U.S. Centers for Disease Control (CDC).* The CDC acts as a worldwide clearinghouse for health and disease information; it is a central source for information when needed, from routine queries to tracking the spread of epidemics. This same clearinghouse function is needed to collect and assess information on disparate cyberspace security incidents.

*Underwriters' Laboratory.* It may be possible to create an institution for the testing and evaluation of the security provisions of telecommunications and other infrastructure software and systems. Perhaps, eventually, systems that don't have this "seal of approval" would not be allowed to interconnect to the infrastructure.

## Key R&D Suggestions

The following are some key research and development suggestions made during the course of group deliberations.

• *Study "distributable secure adaptable architectures"*

Although much research has been done on secure operating systems for individual computers or workstations, new advances are needed for systems that are inherently distributable (over telecommunication links and networks, over geographic distances, among disparate groups) and secure and adaptable. This topic was meant as a theme for a research program, not just an individual project.

• *Study "rapid recovery" strategies and systems*

If any link or node might be disabled by a perpetrator, but could be restored in milliseconds, or at most seconds or minutes, and if the system in addition had considerable redundancy -- then perhaps that would suffice for most systems and applications.

• *Study "understanding and managing complex systems"*

The information systems controlling our national infrastructure have millions of interacting components. We need a better science of complex systems, or at least tools for helping to understand their dynamic operation and vagaries.

• *Study the design of processes for developing secure software systems*

We need an engineering discipline devoted to the design and implementation of secure information systems.

• *Study the concept of a Minimal Essential Information Infrastructure (MEII)*

Among the questions needing study are: What are the essential services the infrastructure must protect and carry? What kinds of functionality must be guaranteed? What is the appropriate communications architecture? What management structure should be used? How do we prototype and exercise the system?

• *Study the MEII functionality for various segments of our society*

Research should be undertaken to ascertain the minimum amount of information infrastructure that would sustain our society for limited periods of time. Such a study would allow estimates to be generated of the minimum essential communication capacity that would be needed in an emergency, as a function of time. These estimates would in turn inform the studies of an MEII (see above).

• *Study the analogy of "biological diversity" for complex information systems*

Biologists have long extolled the virtues of biological diversity. The government may be called upon to mandate that sufficient dissimilarity be engineered into critical systems. Without such intervention, the market is tending toward uniformity in system components to achieve savings from mass production, replication, training, and documentation.

• *Study the biological immune system metaphor for software*

The means by which the human immune system identifies "intruders" and attacks them seems to be an attractive metaphor for software mechanisms that might perform similar functions within a computer network.

• *Study "dynamic diversity" in infrastructure information systems*

Can an information system self-modify periodically so that attacks that work on one portion of it won't work on others, or ones that worked at one time won't work subsequently?

• *Replace software with firmware?*

Attacks frequently modify software controlling infrastructure systems, e.g., to plant Trojan horses or insinuate viruses. Could significant portions of key infrastructure systems be replaced by firmware (e.g., in read-only memories) that would not be amenable to this form of attack?

- *Study the ability to "sterilize" data passing through our telecommunications systems*

Billions of bits of data pass through our national information infrastructure each second, carrying information about individual citizens. The National Security Agency (NSA) is precluded from collecting information about U.S. citizens, even in an IW crisis. Could key data flows be "sterilized" or "sanitized" by computer hardware and/or software in such a manner that the NSA could help monitor and track perpetrators in cyberspace without violating these laws?

- *Study the ability to reengineer or retrofit legacy information systems to enhance their security*

Even if new operating systems or communication protocols were developed to enhance system security, there are thousands of legacy systems throughout the national information infrastructure that would not be affected for years. Is it possible to create "wrappers" or other technology that could be retrofitted into existing legacy systems to significantly improve their security?

- *Sponsor development of an aircraft-like "black box" recording device*

Could a "black box" recording device be developed, to be attached to key nodes or links of cyberspace systems, that would record every transaction passing through that node or link during the last $n$ minutes? That record would be invaluable in tracing the source of incidents, whether they were accidental or deliberately perpetrated.

- *Sponsor development of software or hardware that would record tamper-proof audit trails for information systems*

Many audit trails are merely data recorded into a file for later analysis. If a perpetrator gains root access to a system, he or she can tamper with the audit trail to remove any indication of the perpetrator's presence and activities. How should systems create tamper-proof audit trails that can become accurate records of system activity?

- *Develop software that can perform real-time pattern detection as an aid to attack assessment*

Research should be conducted to advance the capabilities of real-time pattern detection systems, since they form a vital component of any information security program.

# Acknowledgments

The conduct of an exercise involving approximately 60 senior-level participants requires substantial planning and support. First, we are grateful to Dr. Howard Frank of DARPA for his enthusiastic support of this enterprise. His focus and intensity are infectious. We also received administrative support from Michael A. Papillo of Houston Associates, Inc.

Our preparations for this exercise required cooperation and support from a number of RAND staff members who actively participated in walk-throughs of revised scenarios, full-scale dry runs of the exercise, and critiquing sessions. RAND participants in the various activities leading up to, and including, the March 23 exercise included Steven Bankes, James Bonomo, Francis Fukuyama, Eugene Gritton, Richard Hundley, Richard Mesic, Roger Molander, Kevin O'Connell, John Schrader, and Peter Wilson.

We are deeply appreciative of the time and active participation given by the exercise attendees, listed in Appendix A. An additional measure of participation was given by the group leaders--Lawrence Druffel, David Farber, Barry Horton, Robert Kahn, and CAPT Richard O'Neill--who exercised needed leadership over groups of disparate, knowledgable and animated discussants.

Serena Bolton of RAND's Washington D.C. office provided administrative support and acted as a clearinghouse for all the activities, invitations, RSVPs, luncheon and conference room arrangements, and multiple drafts of scenarios required. As usual, Guido (Yogi) Ianiero of RAND's D.C. office provided excellent oversight and control over the local arrangements for the exercise.

# 1. Introduction

"The Day After..." exercise methodology, developed over the past several years under the leadership of Roger Molander, has proven useful in eliciting thinking about complex strategic issues from groups of up to about 60 individuals. The exercises are also useful in "awareness building"--exposing participants to the possible ramifications of current trends, and options for altering those trends. For examples of previous uses of this methodology to explore the national security policy implications of the continued diffusion of nuclear weapons capabilities, see Millot, Molander and Wilson (1993); Mesic, Molander and Wilson (1995); Molander, Wilson, Mesic and Gardiner (1994); and Molander, Riddile and Wilson (1995). A recent application of the methodology to issues of strategic information warfare is presented in Molander, Riddile and Wilson (1996).

The U.S. Defense Advanced Research Projects Agency (DARPA) is interested in understanding strategies for the investment of research and development funds for securing the U.S. information infrastructure against "information warfare" (IW) attacks. (As Roger Molander put it, tongue in cheek, during his opening remarks at the exercise described in this report: "OK, you guys built the ARPAnet, which has become the Internet; now fix it!") A variety of recent studies (e.g., Hundley and Anderson, 1995) have documented the web of interrelated information systems comprising the national information infrastructure and its heavy dependence on the public switched telephone network. These systems are attacked every day by hackers worldwide and, less commonly but more insidiously, by trusted insiders, organized groups, commercial organizations, intelligence agencies, and other agencies of foreign governments. As our society becomes more dependent on this information infrastructure, concern rises about what strategies and technology might best be employed to substantially strengthen the infrastructure against deliberate attacks.

## The Purpose of This Exercise

The purpose of this particular exercise was "to conduct an exercise informing ARPA staff and selected representatives of the user community of the principal features of (defensive) information warfare (IW) and identifying for participants

2

the future demands that IW may place on ARPA information technology programs."[1]  Dr. Howard Frank of DARPA's Information Technology Office acted as the project monitor.

In subsequent discussions with Dr. Frank and among RAND staff, we referred to the exercise purpose as helping inform DARPA's investment strategy for research and development on the integrity and reliability of information systems on which the security and safety of the nation depends.

## The Scenario and Methodology Used for This Exercise

The original "The Day After..." exercise methodology used a three-step process: (1) preparing a memo to a senior government executive regarding problems occurring about five years in the future, in the early stages of a crisis; (2) addressing additional problems several days to a week later, as the crisis worsens; and (3) preparation of a memo "today" (i.e., 1996) discussing measures that should be taken now to avoid problems such as those described in steps 1 and 2.[2]  The diagram used to illustrate this process in previous exercises is shown in Fig. 1.1.

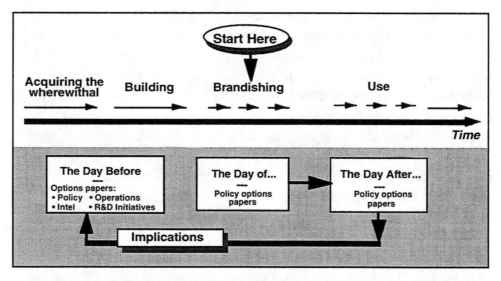

Fig. 1.1 -- "Classic" Three-Step Day After Exercise Methodology

---

[1] From the Project Description, August 25, 1995.  At the time of its writing, DARPA was referred to as ARPA.  In this report, when quoting original materials we use the terminology of those materials.

[2] See the research reports cited in the first paragraph of this section for descriptions of previous exercises using this three-step exercise methodology.

In several dry runs of the DARPA exercise, conducted using RAND staff both in Santa Monica and in Washington DC, we determined that participants became frustrated in steps 1 and 2 because there was little that could be done in the short term to ameliorate or halt the series of cyberspace-based attacks on the U.S. infrastructure. Participants also felt that there was too little time left in the exercise to discuss possible R&D programs that could be instituted today to prevent or greatly reduce such attacks in the future. For these reasons, we decided to modify the exercise so that it contained just two steps: (1) IW attacks occurring five years in the future; and (2) a discussion of what could be done beginning today to cope better with those future attacks. Figure 1.2 shows the revised exercise methodology.

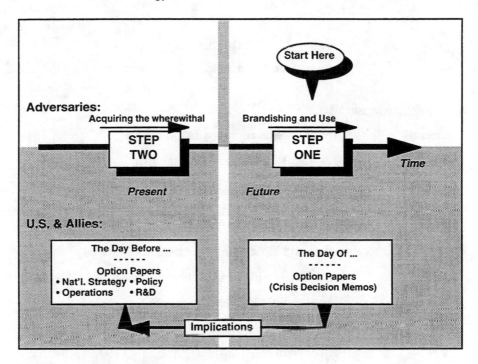

**Fig. 1.2 -- Revised Two-Step Day After Exercise Methodology**

A second dry run using this new methodology proved successful. Participants developed heightened awareness of the problems that could be encountered in the future in Step 1, but then had ample time left to discuss R&D measures in the new Step 2. Because the purpose of this exercise was to develop R&D strategies, this new two-step approach was clearly superior for our purposes.

We began with an existing scenario of cyberspace attacks on U.S. infrastructure used in a previous exercise[3] and tuned and expanded the cyberspace attacks for our particular purposes. We wanted to illustrate the diversity of infrastructure systems dependent on "cyberspace" that might be subject to attack, from transportation control systems to power control to key financial systems. Since the participants for this exercise were to be technologically sophisticated, we added some indications of *how* these attacks might be performed, to increase their believability and counter any possible reactions that "that couldn't possibly happen!".

The set of cyberspace incidents we evolved for the scenario used in this exercise is shown in Table 1.1.

**Table 1.1**

**Cyberspace Incidents Used in Scenario**

### Year 2000 background

| | |
|---|---|
| general | software agents roaming net and Web |
| 1999 | MEII discussed but not yet established |
| 1998 | electronic "looting" of Saudi Arabian bank ($1.2 billion) |
| 1999 | attempted placement of Trojan horse in AB-330 flight control software |
| 1999 | sniffers and logic bombs in Israeli C2 systems |
| general | electronic "looting" of U.S. and European banks by Russians |
| 1998 | computer virus in software causes Yen crisis in Japan |
| 1998-99 | Infonet Threat Center established in U.S. |
| 1999 | flight control software alert regarding U.S. commercial aircraft |

### The Crisis - Step 1

| | |
|---|---|
| 2000 May 11 | power in Cairo (90%) out for several hours -- perpetrator uncertain |
| 2000 May 11 | public switched telephone network (PSTN), massive failure in Riyadh, Saudi Arabia |
| 2000 May 11 | PSTN, Ft. Lewis, WA, mass dialing attack |
| 2000 May 11 | Saudi PSTN, apparent "trap door" in switching code |

---

[3] See Molander, Riddile and Wilson (1996).

| | |
|---|---|
| 2000 May 13 | control malfunction, Aramco refinery, Saudi Arabia -- perpetrator uncertain |
| 2000 May 14 | control malfunction, Bundesbahn train crash, Germany -- perpetrator uncertain |
| 2000 May 16 | sniffers, Bank of England funds transfer system |
| 2000 May 16 | power grid for Rhein Main airbase, Germany, fails |
| 2000 May 17 | non-governmental organization "Consortium for Planetary Peace" mobilization via Internet and other media |
| 2000 May 18 | PSTN in Delaware and Maryland fails -- affects air traffic control at Dover AFB |

### Continuing Crisis - Step 1

| | |
|---|---|
| 2000 May 20 | Automated Teller Machine networks malfunction in Georgia |
| 2000 May 20 | CNN off air for 12 minutes; issues special report |
| 2000 May 20 | worm, corrupting data in Time Phased Force Deployment List (TPFDL) |
| 2000 May 22 | flight control software malfunction; AB-340; plane crash at O'Hare |
| 2000 May 22 | recommendation that all late-model AB-340 and -330s be grounded |
| 2000 May 22 | TV signal in Saudi Arabia replaced by other broadcast |
| 2000 May 23 | PSTN, Saudi, fails; trap doors similar to earlier Saudi PSTN failure |
| 2000 May 23 | full-scale IW attack at CONUS military bases involved in deployment |
| 2000 May 23 | Chicago Commodity Exchange subjected to electronic manipulation |
| 2000 May 23 | PSTN failed, Wash./Baltimore area, similar to Saudi PSTN failure |

## The Conduct of the Exercise

The exercise was held on Saturday morning, March 23, 1996, in RAND's Washington, D.C. offices. After a plenary introductory session to review the scenario and some recent developments, approximately 60 participants were placed into five groups of about 12 persons each to discuss the Step 1 scenario. The agenda for the exercise is shown in Table 1.2.

**Table 1.2**

**Agenda for Exercise**

Saturday, March 23, 1996

| | |
|---|---|
| 0800-0900 | Complementary coffee, tea, rolls, informal get-acquainted discussions among participants |
| 0900-0930 | Welcome to RAND (David Gompert); introductory remarks (Howard Frank); situation briefing (Roger Molander); breakout into five groups |
| 0930-1020 | Working groups on Step 1 |
| 1020-1100 | Plenary session: groups debrief on Step 1 findings and recommendations |
| 1100-1300 | Working groups on Step 2; working lunch served |
| 1300-1400 | Plenary session: groups debrief on Step 2 findings and recommendations |
| 1400 | Conclusion of exercise |

As can be seen in the above agenda, we left two hours for the new Step 2 discussions, plus an hour for a plenary debriefing of the groups, to emphasize the focus on a current R&D agenda that can address future cyberspace insecurities.

In Step 1, participants were told to act as members of "a technical tiger team advising the Secretary of Defense and the Director of ARPA, in a time-urgent process. The group's task is to revise a draft memo to the SECDEF in preparation for the ARPA Director's meeting with the SECDEF scheduled for a few hours hence."[4]

In Step 2, participants were brought back to the "very near future--say the late spring of 1996." They were told that they were "again in the role of a top advisor to the Director of ARPA, preparing him for a meeting with the Secretary of Defense on a national R&D investment strategy for information systems security and related issues."[5]

A list of all participants is provided in Appendix A. The complete scenario and instructions given to all participants are available in Appendix B. The Step 1

---

[4] From the Step 1 scenario instructions. See Appendix B for the complete scenario.
[5] From the Step 2 scenario instructions. See Appendix B.

materials were mailed to participants a week before the exercise. Step 2 materials were handed to them on the day of the exercise at the beginning of their Step 2 group discussion.

The following section contains findings and research suggestions resulting from the groups' deliberations.

# 2. Findings and Research Suggestions

The format of the exercise, described in the previous section, lends itself naturally to two types of observations and findings: those from Step 1, involving short-term actions that can be taken to reduce or ameliorate a set of cyberspace incidents in progress; and those from Step 2 regarding longer-term research and development initiatives that might prevent or greatly reduce the likelihood of such incidents occurring in the future. We present below the key findings and recommendations from group deliberations of steps 1 and 2, concentrating on new observations arising from the discussions, rather than ideas presented in the draft memos given to the participants to stimulate their discussion. The materials presented in this section result both from the group presentations at the plenary sessions and from notes taken by RAND observers who monitored the deliberations of each individual group.

## Step 1. Observations and Findings

At the conclusion of their deliberations regarding the Step 1 incidents occurring in the year 2000, the five groups presented the following observations and findings. In what follows, we have edited their remarks to omit obvious and redundant observations, concentrating on items that might affect DARPA research and development investment initiatives.

In the following discussion, we do not rigidly follow the structure of the "Memo to the SECDEF" in Step 1 of the scenario, because the issues raised there are primarily oriented toward "consciousness-raising" among the participants. Since the scenario in the year 2000 is hypothetical, so are the explicit recommendations made in response to it. We concentrate instead on broader observations about the state of U.S. information vulnerability in the year 2000 and on the tradeoffs and compromises that might be required to deal with attacks on that vulnerability.

### *"Safe havens" should be developed as a fallback means for systems when under attack*

The information systems supporting our nation's infrastructure have become increasingly interconnected during the past several decades. Regional power grids now exchange information and signals more substantially than before; the more than 1500 telecommunication companies providing public-switched telephone service share a common signalling system; and financial trading and exchange systems are linked worldwide with real-time networks. Because of these interdependencies, a vulnerability in one portion of a system can be used to exploit, disrupt, or deny service in other portions--at times geographically remote from the original source of entry.

A possible solution strategy to this problem is to configure these infrastructure systems so that they can quickly be isolated into self-sufficient regional systems. If, in a matter of seconds or minutes, the energy grids or telecommunication systems could be isolated into smaller units, the resulting smaller units might become safe havens protected from remote attack. At a later safe time, the units might be reassembled into an interconnected system. (See the suggestion on the use of "human firewalls" to oversee this reconnection process, under the subhead "Operational aspects of security..." below.)

It was also mentioned that key portions of the infrastructure should have backup repositories of software code (e.g., for telecommunication switches) positioned locally, stored in a manner in which such code can be verified as authentic and accurate. This code could be used for "rebaselining" systems that may have been corrupted. Its local storage is important in case the system in question has been disconnected from other systems, which might prevent downloading the code from a central repository.

## Tactical warning/attack assessment (TW/AA) is an important concept for cyberspace security

There was considerable discussion (prompted by the draft memo to the SECDEF that was part of the Step 1 materials) regarding the concepts of tactical warning and attack assessment.[6] It was agreed that TW/AA is important, and that there is currently little infrastructure in place to perform these activities.

The main reaction was "Who's in charge?". For TW/AA to be successful, there must be a clearinghouse (a "National IW Center"?) to collect, collate, and uncover patterns in cyberspace attacks that span systems in all key infrastructures: transportation, power, finance, communication, defense, and so

---

[6] Tactical warning provides information about an attack in progress; attack assessment determines the extent and characteristics of an attack, including information on targets, consequences, and perpetrators.

forth. At present, there is no agency or entity that is mandated/empowered to collect this information, much less process it.

It was noted that, if such a center existed, it would need software tools to distinguish coordinated attacks from uncoordinated ones.

One possible activity of such a coordinating center would be to design and implement "trigger levels" of activity that would cause alerts to be broadcast to key parts of the U.S. information infrastructure. These alerts might be analogous to the DoD "DEFCON" levels used to represent the state of alert for Defense organizations.

## Operational aspects of security (dealing with people, procedures, regulations) are vitally important to any solution

Although this exercise was focused on R&D initiatives of the type DARPA typically supports, there was considerable discussion of "operational" aspects of security that may be less amenable to R&D, but are deemed vitally important to any overall security posture. It was clear that issues related to people, procedures, regulations, training, education, and so on were a critical adjunct to any successful security technology initiative.

The following operational aspects were specifically mentioned:

*The concept of "cyberspace hot pursuit" needs attention.* We need software tools to aid in the backtracing of incidents, to discover the perpetrator. As such backtracing begins within the U.S. but then crosses country borders, we need clear laws and regulations stating which U.S. or international agencies are authorized to conduct such "cyberspace pursuits", what cooperation should be expected from foreign governments and organizations, and what might be done (in real time, if possible) to disable the means by which the perpetrator is instigating the incidents.

*We need procedures for the prepositioning of backup systems and software.* As mentioned above, the concept of "safe havens" in information systems was discussed, along with the related idea of prepositioning verifiably accurate software (and possibly hardware) for rebaselining corrupted systems. Are there standard procedures that can be developed and used for such baselining? Is each portion of the infrastructure responsible for prepositioning needed systems components, or is some more central organization and coordination desirable?

*"Red teams" are needed to test system defenses.* The groups tended to concur that active testing of system defenses is an important means for assessing system

security. The pioneering tests by the Defense Information Systems Agency (DISA) and the Air Force Information Warfare Center (AFIWC) at Kelly Air Force Base are examples of such testing. The testing concept should be expanded to cover all key national information infrastructure systems. Among the questions needing attention are: What agencies should do the testing? Under what auspices? Would such testing be voluntary or mandatory? What safeguards are needed to protect against unintentional damage or denial of service in these infrastructures as the result of tests? What are the possible legal liabilities as a result of such tests?

*Map the networks.* Cyberspace is a loose concept describing interconnected information systems, with the Internet and the telephone system (PSTN) on which it depends as key--but certainly not the only--components. We need maps of the interconnections among the networks of cyberspace to resolve a number of questions, such as: How do energy grid control systems depend on the PSTN? If a perpetrator appears to be linking into the networks from Iran, or North Korea, or wherever, what are the routes that he or she may take, and can they be blocked? Some agency(ies) should be tasked with maintaining an updated map of the tens of thousands of links and interrelationships and interdependencies among key networks. A subsequent question then arises: Would that map then be widely available to inform discussions of cyberspace security, or classified so that only a select few could access it?

*Personal ID verification systems should be employed.* Participants felt it was important to employ such systems on all links into the infrastructure, including access through dial-in maintenance ports. In this way perpetrators may have an additional hurdle to cross, and an audit trail can be maintained to assign responsibility or blame for incidents.

*The concept of "human firewalls" should be considered in an emergency.* As systems are decomposed into "safe havens" (see above) when an attack is imminent, or during an attack, it might be possible to insert a human as an intelligent verification device to pass judgment before various people and systems are allowed to obtain access to critical nodes and links in the infrastructure.

*A "two-person rule" might be used for critical decisions or system changes.* Just as firing a nuclear missile requires the cooperation of (at least) two individuals, we should consider the advantages (weighed against additional costs and impediments) of requiring two persons to authorize and allow any key change to critical system software, or to implement a decision regarding critical links or nodes. This idea would require considerable analysis to see if it could be practical. See also the discussion of the need for research on the design of secure information systems, below. The "two-person rule" might be a part of the procedures for secure system design and implementation.

*Consider better pay and status for critical system operators.* Personnel might then be less vulnerable to bribes, and less likely to become disgruntled or disaffected. It is widely understood that the trusted insider poses the greatest threat to critical information systems.

### Some notable quotations recorded during Step 1 deliberations

We thought the following comments added information and insight to the proceedings, and were worthy of retention.

> *"If the power system is at risk, everything is at risk."*

> > Many felt that the power system was critical to literally every other component of the infrastructure.

> *"Corrupting compilers is a very powerful, invidious attack."*

> > Control of compilers is a key component of an overall secure process for software development.

> *"There are several examples already where perpetrators have spent 18 months inserting trapdoors, etc., into financial software before beginning to steal money."*

> > Carefully orchestrated and planned attacks are being seen, not just hackers doing their thing.

> *"The U.S. has two main tasks (when under cyberspace attack): (1) recover from what has occurred; and (2) prevent what has not yet occurred."*

> *"Consider putting encryption on all critical control links (e.g., in the power system, the FAA, ...)*

## Step 2. Observations and Findings

Step 2 of the scenario involved the editing and development of a memorandum to the Secretary of Defense regarding steps that could be initiated "today" to reduce U.S. vulnerability to cyberspace-based attacks in the future. Some of the observations of Step 1, above, were reiterated. Perhaps the most interesting new observation dealt with analogies the U.S. government might consider in considering its posture and relationship with industry in working toward better cyberspace security. Three specific analogies were mentioned:

• *Automobile safety regulations*

The U.S. government, in cooperation with the auto industry, created regulations that raised the safety level of automobiles. These regulations also raised awareness of safety issues within the U.S. populace in general. The safety and security of cyberspace is now in a situation analogous to that of the automobile industry many years ago. With appropriate regulations, the market could be influenced in a substantial way. This is important because market forces will ultimately have the major influence on the safety and security of U.S. information systems.

• *The U.S. Centers for Disease Control (CDC)*

The CDC acts as a worldwide clearinghouse for health and disease information; it is a central source for information when needed, from routine queries to tracking the spread of epidemics. This same clearinghouse function is needed to collect and assess information on disparate cyberspace security incidents.

• *Underwriters' Laboratory*

It may be possible to create an institution for the testing and evaluation of the security provisions of telecommunications and other infrastructure software and systems. Perhaps, eventually, systems that don't have this "seal of approval" would not be allowed to interconnect to the infrastructure. It is an open question, however, if the safety and security of complex operating systems and application programs comprising millions of lines of source code could in fact be so tested. The evolution of software systems (multiple versions and releases, new system components, etc.) may be too rapid for this task to be accomplished in reasonable time or at reasonable expense.

## R&D Investment Suggestions

We believe the following are the most important specific research and development suggestions made during the course of Step 2 deliberations.

### • *Study "distributable secure adaptable architectures"*

The group that coined the phrase "distributable secure adaptable architectures" believed each word in the phrase was important. Although much research has been done on secure operating systems for individual computers or workstations, new advances are needed for systems that are inherently distributable (over telecommunication links and networks, over geographic distances, among disparate groups). These systems should be secure and adaptable, because rigid system solutions are bypassed or trashed as the environment in which they must work evolves. They must be architectural, dealing with all system levels, rather than "silver bullets" meant to solve narrow specific problems. This topic was meant as a theme for a research program, not just an individual project.

### • *Study "rapid recovery" strategies and systems*

Participants despaired of the design and implementation of verifiably secure information systems throughout the nation's infrastructure--at least in their lifetimes. But perhaps even near-absolute security would be much less necessary if systems were designed for rapid recovery. If any link or node might be disabled by a perpetrator, but could be restored in milliseconds, or at most seconds or minutes, and if the system in addition had considerable redundancy -- then perhaps that would suffice for most systems and applications. What portions of the infrastructure might be amenable to such a solution? How might systems be designed with rapid recovery from malevolent (or inadvertent) acts as a design criterion?

### • *Study "understanding and managing complex systems"*

The information systems controlling our national infrastructure are some of the most complex systems ever designed. They have millions of interacting components. Often, each node is controlled by millions of lines of code. We need a better science of complex systems, or at least tools for helping to understand their dynamic operation and vagaries. Among the tools that were suggested at the exercise were:

- *Data probes and selective sampling* as a means of ascertaining the health and vitality of a system during its operation;

- *Intelligent modeling tools* for representing such complexity at various levels of abstraction;

- *Tools for the visualization of information flows*. With proper visualization could abnormal patterns of activity be detected before they became destructive?

- *Interactive and multiple-scale global analysis*. How can analysis be conducted at various levels of the system, interactively during system operation?

## • *Study the design of processes for developing secure software systems*

Through the efforts of the Software Engineering Institute, among others, a "science" of software engineering is slowly emerging. They are developing standards for assessing the level of maturity of software development groups. We need comparable processes and an engineering discipline devoted to the design and implementation of secure information systems. Such processes must include a variety of procedures to ensure the validity of the compiler being used and protect access to it, which may require a "two-man rule" for making critical system changes (see "Operational aspects...", above), and numerous other procedural and technical safeguards. An entire science and discipline of secure system development is needed.

## • *Study the concept of a Minimal Essential Information Infrastructure (MEII)*

The scenario materials given to the participants presented for their consideration the concept of a Minimal Essential Information Infrastructure. Groups generally supported exploration of the idea, and encouraged study of

- *the essential services it must protect and carry.* How many are there? What are their information demands?

- *the functionality that must be guaranteed.* Participants stressed attention to functionality, rather than becoming absorbed in the "nuts and bolts" of specific hardware and system components.

- *the appropriate telecommunications architecture.* Do existing telecommunication systems provide the appropriate redundancy and architecture, or are alternative designs needed?

- *a global management structure.* We come back to the question: Who's in charge? Is an MEII managed in a decentralized manner, or centrally? What regulations and guidelines govern its use?

- *prototyping and exercising the system.* It was widely understood that an MEII could not be created and "put on the shelf" for use in emergencies only. The information environment is much too dynamic for such a warehoused system to remain viable. It must be used regularly to remain relevant.

Some felt that encouraging diversity in infrastructure systems (of both paths and system architecture) was more important than attempting to design or develop an MEII. Others stated that "DoD, for cost reasons, will have to fall back on a reduced functionality system like MilStar, rather than attempting to secure, or duplicate, portions of the nation's existing telecommunications system." It was unclear, however, whether such satellite links could be extended to cover the communications required by non-Defense portions of critical national infrastructures.

## • *Study the minimum essential functionality for various segments of our society*

This question is related to the previous topic. Research should be undertaken to ascertain the minimum amount of information infrastructure that would sustain our society for limited periods of time. If the energy system could only provide half the normal power, would that suffice for a week? Would 2/3 of banking systems suffice; if so, for how long? If 1/4 the air traffic control systems were inoperable for 48 hours, could air transportation continue, and if so with what throughput compared to normal? Such a study would allow estimates to be generated of the minimum essential communication capacity that would be needed in an emergency, as a function of time. These estimates would in turn inform the studies of an MEII (see above).

## • *Study the analogy of "biological diversity" for complex information systems*

Considerable concern was expressed at the exercise about the limited diversity in our key infrastructure systems. Most telephone switches are made by one of only a few companies (e.g., Nortel, Siemens, AT&T), and these switches are almost exclusively based on the Unix or VMS operating systems. Most Internet nodes run common versions of the Unix operating system. The telephone signaling system uses the Internet's SMTP message transfer protocol. And so on. Once perpetrators discover a flaw in such systems, that flaw can be quickly exploited in thousands of copies of that system component. Biologists have long extolled the virtues of biological diversity, so that crops such as corn, wheat, etc. are not genetically identical and subject to the same diseases or infestations. In the same way, government may be called upon to mandate that sufficient dissimilarity be engineered into critical systems. Without such intervention, the market is tending toward uniformity in system components to achieve savings from mass production, replication, training, and documentation.

## • *Consider the biological immune system metaphor for software*

The Step 2 draft memo handed to group discussants mentioned as a possible research idea the concept of modeling system defenses on the tactics used by the human immune system to discover and immobilize "intruders". As described in Hundley and Anderson (1995):

> The biological agents providing the active defense portion of the immune system employ certain critical capabilities: the ability to distinguish "self" from "nonself"; the ability to create and transmit recognition templates and killer mechanisms throughout the organism; and the ability to evolve defenses as the "threat" changes.
>
> Software agents providing a cyberspace active defense analogue to these biological antibodies would need the same capabilities.
>
> The message of this metaphor is clear: Cyberspace security would be enhanced by active defenses capable of evolving over time.

Some existing research is underway based on this metaphor, for example, see Forrest *et al.* (1994) and Kephart (1994). Discussants at the exercise were intrigued by the concept and recommended further exploration of its possibilities.

## • *Study "dynamic diversity" in infrastructure information systems*

A security problem with existing infrastructure systems is their stability and consistency. Once a flaw is discovered, it can be exploited for months and on multiple instances of that system throughout the country. Groups talked about the possibility of dynamic diversity, wherein software at all levels of these systems modified itself frequently in a way that didn't affect functionality, but that could foil attempts to exploit known security flaws. Perhaps if file names changed, the location of software modules moved, alternate protocols were used, and so on, it would preclude broad attacks on multiple identical system components. Is such dynamic diversity possible, while retaining the ability to perform maintenance, upgrades, training, and other activities that depend on stability in systems? The related topic of a system performing dynamic self-configuring around corrupted elements was also mentioned; this is another biologically-related metaphor which recurred in group discussions.

### • *Replace software with firmware?*

Software is modifiable. Firmware (instructions burned into read-only memory (ROM) or related memory devices) is much less so. Can software in critical systems be replaced by firmware so that it cannot be "hacked" by intruders? If so, which systems are amenable to this approach? How would the security improvements of this approach weigh against the greater difficulty of upgrading and maintaining--e.g., by the changing of ROM chips rather than remotely downloading software--the instructions controlling system behavior?

### • *Is it possible to "sterilize" data passing through our telecommunications systems?*

Billions of bits of data pass through our national information infrastructure each second. Some of those bits represent information about individual citizens' login and password combinations, social security and credit card numbers, account information, health status, and innumerable other sensitive information items. Our nation has superb communications monitoring tools, housed primarily in the National Security Agency. However, the NSA is precluded by law from collecting information about U.S. citizens. When incidents of "information warfare" are being waged against U.S. systems, could key data flows be "sterilized" or "sanitized" by computer hardware and/or software in such a manner that the NSA could help monitor and track perpetrators in cyberspace without violating these laws? This topic was raised during exercise discussions. We have not studied all the relevant laws and regulations to assess whether such sterilization measures would allow the power of NSA's analyses to be brought to bear on telecommunications involving U.S. citizens, but perhaps the topic merits further investigation. If so, what kinds of pattern detection and replacement algorithms would suffice to accomplish this goal?

### • *Study the ability to reengineer or retrofit legacy information systems to enhance their security*

There are thousands of existing information systems and components supporting the national information infrastructure, including individual PSTN switches, pipeline control systems, the air traffic control system, Internet routers, and so on. It is clearly not possible, in the next decade or two, to redesign and reprogram all these systems to enhance their security significantly. Is it possible, however, to retrofit these systems with special hardware/software devices for greater security? An analogy might be the "TCP Wrapper" technology pioneered by Wietse Venema[7] and others that is used as a software retrofit on a key Internet protocol. Are other security-enhancing "wrappers" possible in other circumstances? The entire topic of retrofitting existing systems could use substantial R&D if significant progress on infrastructure security is to be made on any reasonable time scale.

## • *Sponsor development of an aircraft-like "black box" recording device*

When a cyberspace security incident happens, it is often not detected in real time, and the trail back to the perpetrator becomes lost. Could a "black box" recording device be developed, to be attached to key nodes or links of cyberspace systems, that would record every transaction passing through that node or link during the last $n$ minutes (where $n=5$ or 10, for example)? If so, that record would be invaluable in tracing the source of incidents, whether they are accidental or deliberately perpetrated. Thousands of such systems would be required to cover key links or nodes; could they be made robust, inexpensive, and ultra-reliable?

## • *Sponsor development of devices that would record tamper-proof audit trails for information systems*

This concept is related to the previous one. A variety of critical infrastructure systems retain some level of audit trail of system activity, to help in diagnosing problems. Many such audit trails are merely data recorded into a file for later analysis. If a perpetrator gains root access to a system, he or she can tamper with the audit trail to remove any indication of the perpetrator's presence and activities. How should systems create tamper-proof audit trails that can become accurate records of system activity? Since it is impossible for many systems to retain a record of *all* activity over lengthy periods of time, such tamper-proof audit trails may well need to be "FIFO queues" (first-in first-out), where the newest information recorded pushes out the oldest information because of limited recording space.

## • *Develop software that can perform real-time pattern detection as an aid to attack assessment*

Systems are currently under development, and being fielded, that monitor for suspicious or abnormal activity in real time during a system's operation.

---

[7] See Venema (1992).

Examples include SRI's Next Generation Intrusion Detection Expert System (NIDES)[8] and work at the Air Force Information Warfare Center. Research should be conducted to evolve the capabilities of such real-time pattern detection systems, since they form a vital component of any information security program. Participants mentioned that neural nets are one appropriate technology to be considered, since they can be self-adapting as patterns of system activity change. We are aware that some existing systems already incorporate both neural-net and rule-based components. These use biological metaphors analogous to those we discussed earlier.

---

[8] Anderson, Fribold and Valdes (1995); Anderson, Lunt, Javitz, Tamaru and Valdes (1995).

# Concluding Remarks

We believe the "Day After..." exercise accomplished its goal. Stimulating discussions on the topic of R&D approaches to cyberspace security were held over five hours by some of the key governmental, university, and private industry resource persons who could contribute most to such a discussion. The exercise scenario seemed believable to participants; we heard no reactions that "Oh, that couldn't happen" (e.g., to the public switched telephone system, the energy system, the transportation system). The scenario focused the discussion on specific problems to be addressed, both with short-term expedients and longer-term R&D strategies.

Sixty participants were about the maximum that could be handled by the facilities and arrangements. If there are five groups of 12 discussants, it takes about an hour for all five groups to debrief and present their findings and observations to the plenary sessions. Two such plenaries, and at least three hours of group discussions (plus a working lunch, an introductory scene-setting session, and concluding remarks) totally absorbed the participants for five hours.

Would we do anything differently, based on this experience? The main lesson is one we have learned, and taken to heart, before: Vital information is gathered in serious walk-throughs and dry runs of the exercise; such activities cannot be shirked. For example, we believe it was crucial to the success of the exercise that the former three steps were cut down to two, and more time was allotted for the final step's discussion of current initiatives that might be undertaken. That insight came directly from the earlier dry runs we conducted.

# Appendix A. List of Participants

A wide variety of representatives from industries, universities, government, and research institutions involved with the U.S. information infrastructure were invited to participate in the March 23 exercise. The resulting participant list is provided below. Names marked with "*" acted as group leaders for the exercise.

### GROUP A

| | |
|---|---|
| Larry Dubois | Defense Advanced Research Projects Agency |
| Howard Frank | Defense Advanced Research Projects Agency |
| Ken Gabriel | Defense Advanced Research Projects Agency |
| Howard Shrobe | Defense Advanced Research Projects Agency |
| Duane Andrews | Defense Science Board representative; Science Applications International Corporation |
| Roger Callahan | Defense Science Board representative; Director, Information Systems Security, OASD(C3I) |
| Mary Dunham | Defense Science Board representative; Special Assistant to DDS&T, CIA |
| * Barry Horton | Office of the Secretary of Defense/C3I |
| Richard Liebhaber | MCI |
| Bruce McConnell | Office of Management and Budget |
| Thomas McDermott | National Security Agency |
| Shukri Wakid | National Institute of Standards and Technology |
| Richard Hundley | RAND observer/recorder |

### GROUP B

| | |
|---|---|
| Randy Garrett | Defense Advanced Research Projects Agency |
| Tom Garvey | Defense Advanced Research Projects Agency |
| David Gunning | Defense Advanced Research Projects Agency |
| Thomas Swartz | Defense Advanced Research Projects Agency |
| John Grimes | Defense Science Board representative; Electrospace Systems Inc. |
| * CAPT Dick O'Neill | Deputy Director, Information Warfare, OASD(C3I) |
| Colin Crook | Citibank NA |
| John Davis | National Computer Security Center, National Security Agency |
| Mike Papillo | Houston Associates, Inc. |
| Jerry Wind | SEI Center for Advanced Studies, University of Pennsylvania |
| Anthony Hearn | RAND observer/recorder |

## GROUP C

| | |
|---|---|
| Bert Hui | Defense Advanced Research Projects Agency |
| Taylor Lawrence | Defense Advanced Research Projects Agency |
| Larry Lynn | Defense Advanced Research Projects Agency |
| Dave Whelan | Defense Advanced Research Projects Agency |
| CAPT William Gravell | Defense Science Board representative; Chief, Information Warfare Division, Joint Staff |
| CAPT David Henry | Defense Science Board representative; Director of Information Warfare, National Security Agency |
| John Lane | Defense Science Board representative; Information Delivery Group, NationsBank |
| Marjory Blumenthal | Computer Science & Telecommunications Board |
| William Griffin | GTE Labs |
| * Robert Kahn | Corporation for National Research Initiatives |
| Robert Meushaw | National Security Agency |
| Ruth David | Deputy Director, Science and Technology, Central Intelligence Agency |
| David Tennenhouse | Massachusetts Institute of Technology |
| Eugene Gritton | RAND observer/recorder |

## GROUP D

| | |
|---|---|
| Gary Koob | Defense Advanced Research Projects Agency |
| Teresa Lunt | Defense Advanced Research Projects Agency |
| Gary Minden | Defense Advanced Research Projects Agency |
| Duane Adams | Defense Advanced Research Projects Agency |
| Donald Latham | Defense Science Board representative; Loral Corporation |
| Alan McLaughlin | Defense Science Board representative; Lincoln Laboratory, Massachusetts Institute of Technology |
| Jerry Tuttle | Defense Science Board representative; Oracle Corporation |
| Gene Cacciamani | Hughes Network Systems |
| * David Farber | University of Pennsylvania |
| Joseph Moorcones | National Security Agency |
| Larry Smarr | National Center for Supercomputing Applications, University of Illinois |
| George Spix | Microsoft Corporation |
| Robert Anderson | RAND observer/recorder |

**GROUP E**

| | |
|---|---|
| Robert Parker | Defense Advanced Research Projects Agency |
| Rob Rosenthal | Defense Advanced Research Projects Agency |
| David Signori | Defense Advanced Research Projects Agency |
| ADM Harry Train (Ret) | Defense Science Board representative; Science Applications International Corporation |
| Wushou Chou | U.S. Treasury Department |
| Brent Greene | Office of Emergency Preparedness Policy |
| Lionel S. Johns | Office of Science and Technology Policy |
| * Larry Druffel | Software Engineering Institute |
| Amar Gupta | Massachusetts Institute of Technology |
| Larry Landweber | Internet Society |
| Robert Pepper | Federal Communications Commission |
| Richard Schaffer | National Security Agency |
| | |
| Roger Molander | RAND observer/recorder |

# Appendix B. Scenario and Instructional Materials Used in Exercise

The following pages contain all of the exercise materials used in the March 23, 1996 exercise.

# The Day After...

## ...in Cyberspace - II (ARPA)

The "Day After..." methodology requires a realistic scenario; however, specific companies, systems, or system components appearing in this scenario are examples only and their appearance implies no unique capability or vulnerability. Attribution to any organization or entity shall not be made as a result of the text contained herein.

## STEP ONE

## RAND

23 March 1996

# TABLE OF CONTENTS

## The Day After...

### ...in Cyberspace - II (ARPA)

| | |
|---|---|
| Methodology | 2 |
| STEP ONE: The Day Of... | |
| Situation Report | 4 |
| Instructions | 16 |
| Memo for the SECDEF | 17 |
| | |
| *(Note: Step Two is provided on site.)* | |
| | |
| STEP TWO: The Day Before... | |
| Instructions | 33 |
| Memo for the SECDEF | 34 |

Robert H. Anderson
Anthony C. Hearn

Eugene Gritton
Richard O. Hundley
Richard F. Mesic
Roger C. Molander
Kevin O'Connell
Peter Wilson

# METHODOLOGY

**"The Day After..."** exercise methodology has been developed to explore new and evolving post-Cold War international security problems, in particular in the realm of new types of strategic warfare.

This version of the exercise methodology is based on a two-step process generally lasting a total of approximately four to five hours.

Participants in the exercises take on the role of advisors to a senior-level decision-maker (or decision-making body) in a group deliberative process akin to a classic time-constrained "pre-meeting" where the principal task is to finalize a document or set of materials (e.g., an issues and options paper) for a formal deliberative/decision-making meeting (such as a National Security Council meeting).

In general, two or more groups (of nominally 6-12 individuals under the leadership of a chairperson) go through the identical exercise at the same time and compare the character and results of their deliberations at the end of each of the steps.

\* \* \*

In this particular application of the methodology--"The Day After...in Cyberspace - II (ARPA)--participlants take on the role of a technical tiger team advising the Secretary of Defense and the Director of ARPA on recommendations to put forth to the President:

(1) on possible short-term technical solutions to a set of pressing cyberspace security problems that emerge in the context of a <u>future</u> political-military crisis (STEP ONE of the exercise) and

(2) on prospective <u>current/near-term</u> R&D-related strategy and policy initiatives that would address existing and projected strategic vulnerabilities in the U.S. defense and national information infrastructures (STEP TWO).

\* \* \*

The exercise process begins (see schematic on the next page) with the tiger team convened to examine a set of critical cyberspace-related technical issues that are manifest on <u>"the day of"</u> (STEP ONE) a significant change in the strategic situation in a crisis in the Persian Gulf set in the year 2000.

The group's STEP ONE task is to revise a draft of a memo from the SECDEF to the President on possible short-term fixes to the pressing cyberspace technical issues that have emerged in this crisis.

In the context of this tasking group, consensus on the text of the memo and recommendations to go forward to the SECDEF is desirable but not necessary. Where consensus cannot be achieved, the group notes and conveys forward the prevailing differences for final decision-making by the Secretary of Defense in consultation with the Director of ARPA.

In <u>"the day before"</u> (STEP TWO) of the exercise, the context changes to the present or near future.

In this more contemporary context, the group is again convened as a team with another time-constrained tasking. Ths group must revise and improve a memo which is going from the Director of ARPA to the Secretary of Defense immediately in advance of a cabinet-level meeting where it is intended that the President decide on a new national R&D initiative investment strategy for information systems security, to be manifest in a set of new initiatives on:

(1) Overall investment strategy,

(2) New operational concepts and practices based on new technological opportunities, and

(3) New R&D initiatives and new R&D priorities

In this second step the group's task is to revise a draft memo from the Director of ARPA to the SECDEF on a recommended set of initiatives.

The objective in this last step is to seek initiatives that would help minimize the prospect that future crises such as that just faced would occur--or, if they do, to mitigate their consequences, and reduce the likelihood that they would ever occur again.

# METHODOLOGY (cont.)

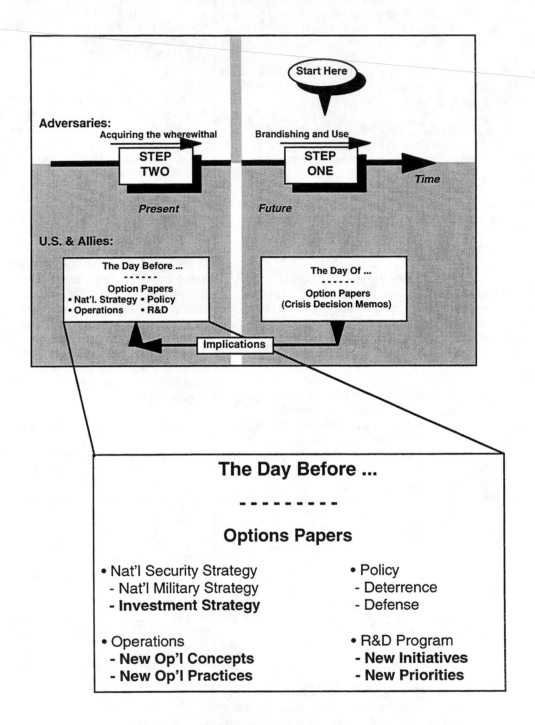

**"The Day After..." Methodology
(Applied to Strategic Information Warfare)**

# STEP ONE: The Day Of...

# SITUATION REPORT

## BACKGROUND

It is now mid-spring in **the year 2000.**

As the Twentieth Century drew to a close, **political changes and continued unrest** in the **Persian Gulf**, in **Pakistan**, in the **Islamic countries of the former Soviet Union**, and across the breadth of **North Africa** had created a new and profoundly troubled region of the world now frequently labeled **"the Islamic Arc of Crisis."**

Adding to U.S. and European concerns about this region was the rising prospect that one or more of the **potential predators** in the region had developed the capacity to **exploit the Global Information Infrastructure (GII) as a field of strategic political-military operations.**

The latter situation has sparked particular **anxiety** in the U.S. about the **safety and security** of **the U.S. National Information Infrastructure (NII)** and **an evolving Defense Information Infrastructure (DII)** (see below).

## MAJOR FEATURES OF THE GII, NII, AND DII

In the 1990s the **Cellular/Wireless Revolution** proceeded apace with the availability of new low and medium earth orbit satellite constellations such as *Iridium* and *Globestar* providing **readily accessible global two-way communications via portable telephones.** It is now estimated that 25% of the North American, European, and Japanese adults routinely carry a cellphone. A similar explosion of cellphone use continues in other major markets.

**The Internet has become a pillar of both the NII and GII.** All countries now have Internet hosts, and it is estimated that 70% of the world's population now lives within a local telephone call of an Internet gateway.

The phenomenon of **the World Wide Web has continued to expand, with over forty million "home pages" of information** providing links to data bases around the world. Many of these home pages include video and voice releases specially designed for consumption by the mass media.

One of the most significant trends of the past decade has been the **growth of electronic commerce.** Current estimates suggest that **a third of all formal U.S. business transactions now occur electronically** using both standardized data interchanges and specialized communications between cooperating companies employing a range of digital encryption standards.

**Attempts by the U.S. government to establish a hardware encryption standard** (successors to the CLIPPER CHIP initiative) **have been thwarted** by lawsuits brought by both citizen groups and software companies.

The NII and GII are also being heavily used by a **new generation of activist groups.** Many such groups are **linked in transnational networks** that address a broad range of environmental, human-rights, and other global issues.

The **Internet** and **World Wide Web** have become **virtual battlegrounds for software "agents" of various types.** Tens of thousands of such agents have been unleashed to roam "the Net" and "the Web" looking for items meeting a profile of interests of their users, or blocking such access.

In 1998 the President decided to allow **the bulk of the Defense Department's "peacetime and administrative communications"** to continue to **rely on the commercial switched telephone and public data systems.** The vast majority of DII communications now pass over the commercial **Public Switched Network (PSN)**, relying on **various levels of encryption** to protect classified information.

During the period from 1995-2000 **various largely unsuccessful attempts** were made **to increase the security of the PSN.** These efforts have been complicated by the fact that **"the PSN" is run and maintained by many competing companies** including cable, cellular, and satellite operators, so that changes are difficult to mandate and place into effect. As a result, other than individual use of end-to-end encryption by cooperating parties, **PSN security in the year 2000 is not much better than that in 1996.**

# SITUATION REPORT (cont.)

The problem is exacerbated by several continuing trends: (1) widespread use of **open, standard systems** whose protocols and internals are well known; (2) cost saving by increased use of **remote maintenance** (e.g., through dial-in ports) in telecom and energy control systems; (3) more **shared trust** among many disparate providers of PSN service; (4) more **frequent changes to PSN software** caused by competition based on new features and facilities among providers.

In 1998 the possibility of the U.S. developing a (national and global) **Minimum Essential Information Infrastructure (MEII)**--to insure that there would be "emergency lanes on the information highway" for a variety of contingencies --became a matter of serious discussion. The principal motivation was the perceived need to establish a **minimum capability** to support prospective **large-scale U.S. and allied force deployment operations.**

While discussion of various MEII architectures and performance criteria continue, **serious development work on an actual MEII has not yet begun.** There remains **broad disagreement on the scope** of such a system with the debate focused on:

  • Protecting **only military and other communications and information systems key to major force deployment operations** vs.

  • Also protecting **other infrastructure information systems more directly impacting the U.S. populace** vs.

  • Also protecting the **information systems of allies and potential coalition partners**

There is also **wide debate about the ability to maintain the viability and effectiveness of any MEII** that could be developed, largely in light of the continued highly dynamic character of the information revolution.

In light of the above environment, in the last few years there has been **rising concern** over the **increasing interdependence** of the **PSN**, the U.S. **electrical power grid**, data networks supporting the **air traffic control system**, the **Global Positioning System** (GPS), and **other key U.S. infrastructure elements.** As a consequence

of this concern, national security, intelligence, and law enforcement agencies in the U.S. (as well as in other nations) are devoting **increased resources** to efforts to **assess and counter both domestic and foreign IW threats.**

# SITUATION REPORT (cont.)

## MAJOR FEATURES OF THE GLOBAL SECURITY ENVIRONMENT

### *Saudi Arabia Under Stress*

Recently there have been **major steps by the Saudi government to open up Saudi society politically, economically, and socially.** New independent television stations are broadcasting and there has been proliferation of direct broadcast satellite receivers and cellular telecommunications systems. All elements of society are making increasing use of a variety of Internet nodes.

The **Saudi monarchy has suffered substantially** from internal dissent and distress since the 1997 death of King Fahd. **A weak successor now struggles to govern both the family and the kingdom,** which is increasingly beset by **growing tensions between an Islamic fundamentalist dissident movement and the "nationalist modernizers"** who currently dominate the Saudi government.

By 1998, much of the **Saudi dissident movement** (especially within the universities) had **coalesced around the goals and objectives of the increasingly influential Campaign for Islamic Renewal and Democracy (CIRD).** This loose transnational CIRD coalition, formed at the 1997 Damascus meeting of Islamic state and non-governmental organizations (NGOs), has become **a prominent force for social and political change** in the **Persian Gulf** region as well as **throughout the Islamic world.**

The CIRD is **very well funded**, principally by North American and European Islamic sources but also in part by domestic sources in Saudi Arabia, Iran, and Pakistan. The **CIRD exploits a variety of modern advanced information and communications technologies** for organizing, fund-raising, media coverage, and building ties to organizations throughout the global Islamic and broader NGO community. Several CIRD chapters are now very **prominent within the North American Islamic community.**

**Oil prices have remained stable throughout the 1990s** which has forced the Saudi Kingdom to make **cutbacks in ambitious domestic and social programs** designed in part to "keep domestic peace."

The Saudi regime's **nervousness about their overall security and financial vulnerability** markedly increased in early 1998 following the revelation that **the Bank of Saudi Arabia had been "looted" of nearly $1.2 billion by a sophisticated electronic attack** which for two months had successfully used "skimming" and other "cyberspace bank robbery" techniques before detection by a British financial security service. The Saudi government later found **strong evidence of both Iranian and Syrian involvement** in the attack.

Adding to the Saudi kingdom's fiscal woes is the broad **consensus within the monarchy and government elites**--strongly opposed by CIRD supporters within Saudi Arabia--that **defense spending must remain high in the face of the increasing military and political power of Iran** (see below).

# SITUATION REPORT (cont.)

## Persia Ascendant

**Iran's power and influence in the Persian Gulf rose dramatically** following the **1997 Iraqi civil war** that erupted in the wake of Saddam Hussein's abrupt departure. As a result of a highly effective Iranian intervention in the civil war, **Iraq is now essentially divided.** A weak post-Baathist central government has been installed in Baghdad while the Kurds in the north and Shiites in the south enjoy virtual autonomy in most matters.

**Iran openly supports radical Islamic fundamentalist groups in almost all of the Gulf states** and trumpets a "pan-Islamic" strategy of building a broad political-military coalition to "resist American and European hegemony in the Islamic world."

Iran's nuclear weapons ambitions are widely acknowledged though there is at present **no evidence that the Iranians have any operational nuclear weapons.** The Iranians continue to maintain that their rapidly growing nuclear infrastructure--which remains under IAEA inspection--is for "nuclear energy alone."

Iran continues to improve its long-range weapons delivery capability which currently includes: (1) 36 **Russian Tu-22M Backfires,** (2) an IRBM force of two dozen **North Korean *Nodong II* missiles,** and (3) an MRBM force of 200-300 ***Nodong I* missiles.**

**Evidence of the extent of development of Iranian IW activity emerged in 1999 in India** when three Indian nationals (including an acknowledged "world class" software writer) were arrested by authorities after penetrating supposedly highly secure Indian defense networks, and in the course of plea-bargaining **confessed to selling Iran "a variety of 21st Century information warfare tools."**

Iran maintains **an uneasy relationship with the CIRD** which has resisted Iranian efforts to convert the coalition to a more fundamentalist Islamic posture. In addition, a number of **CIRD leaders have privately criticized the slow pace of democratization in Iran.** However, intelligence sources report that Iran is channeling funds to some factions within the CIRD coalition.

## Algeria

Popular support for the Algerian military martial law government continued to unravel into 1996, and **in June 1996 a pro-Islamic "colonels' faction" led a coup which took control of the government** in concert with the "Rome coalition" of former government opposition groups. In the fall of 1996, an Islamic government was formally established in a new round of national elections.

In the summer of 1998, relations between Algeria and the U.S. and Europe began to deteriorate as the **new Algerian regime increasingly tilted toward the geo-strategic and political interests of Iran** and military cooperation programs between the two countries became more widespread.

During the summer of 1999, French intelligence services were alerted to the **attempted placement of a computer "Trojan horse" in the latest variant of the AirBus Industries AB-330 flight control software,** apparently by **Algerian agents in France acting under the direction of Iran.** French aviation authorities found that Aerospatiale had been relying upon several Indian software subcontractors which had access to supposedly "secure" source code development and compilers.

## Libya

In November of 1998 while flying to inspect a new chemical weapon facility in southern Libya, **President Qadhafi was severely injured** in a helicopter crash and shortly thereafter retired. In the political turmoil that followed, **a strongly nationalist Islamic government quickly seized power** and consolidated control of the country.

Much to the surprise of many observers, the new Libyan government **moved rapidly to hold elections** and embrace "Islamic democracy." It is now viewed as **one of the CIRD's strongest government supporters** in the effort to build a united democracy-based Islamic political force.

# SITUATION REPORT (cont.)

## Pakistan

In 1997, the **Bhutto regime was overthrown by a military coup** which faulted the government for "political indecisiveness and inadequate military assistance" in the failed "Tet-like" **general uprising in Kashmir in late 1996.**

With the departure of the Bhutto regime, the military-dominated government took on **an increasingly militant Islamic stance** which included **dramatically expanded political-military ties with Iran.**

## Israel and the Arabs

Israel signed **peace agreements with both Syria and Lebanon in 1997.**

In the summer of 1999, the Israeli government began to be subject to (in Mossad's terminology) "a new form of strategic warfare"--a series of **electronic attacks on Israel's military command and control system** by a sophisticated array of **"sniffers" and "logic bombs" of uncertain origin.**

## The Russian Federation

**A strongly "Russian nationalist" regime came to power in the 1996 elections** and moved quickly to consolidate power and influence both within the Federation and in "the near abroad."

In 1997 the Russian military created **a new Radio Electronic Combat Command** which has been charged with the development of "a comprehensive 21st Century offensive and defensive information warfare capability."

The new Russian information warfare effort in part reflected acknowledgment of a continuing domestic problem--**increasingly sophisticated internal "cyberspace banditry" techniques employed by Russian "mafiya" organized crime groups.** While such attacks within Russia have diminished, the groups continue to mount successful attacks on European and American banks (with an estimated gain of over $2 billion in the year 1999 alone). U.S. and European intelligence and law enforcement services strongly suspect that **some of the best Russian "mafiya hacker talent" is now in the pay of the Russian intelligence services.**

## China

**A "tough, pragmatic, and strongly nationalist" leadership has consolidated power in a post-Deng Xiaopeng China** which continues to lead Asia on an upward trajectory of economic growth.

Reflecting ever-increasing Chinese self-confidence, there is now a dominant view among the Chinese political and military leadership **that China should acquire "strategic military power second to none" in the early 21st Century.**

A **new and widely remarked Chinese "21st Century strategic asset"** is the acknowledged skill of a emerging generation of **Chinese computer experts** which provide both the Chinese commercial and banking sectors and the government **with world-class offensive and defensive IW "hacker" capability.**

## Japan

The Japanese government **interest in potential IW threats** was profoundly **heightened after the "Great Yen crisis of 1998"** when the Japanese currency nearly collapsed after a two-day fall of 22%. Only several months after the fact was there sufficient suspicion the massive fall in the Yen had been partially **"induced by a very sophisticated computer virus program"** of which the authors were believed to be an alliance of several **Chinese and other Asian Transnational Criminal Organizations (TCOs).**

## The Koreas

**Kim Jong II continues to maintain control** over the key levers of power in the DPRK although there continue to be internal power struggles around him between various factions in the North Korean elite-- which continues to hold back reunification efforts.

Implementation of the 1994 U.S.-DPRK nuclear "framework" has proceeded in fits and starts, but it continues to be seen as **successful in holding back the North Korean nuclear program.** However, the DPRK maintains a robust indigenous missile development and production program and **an extensive missile export and cooperative development program with Iran.**

# SITUATION REPORT (cont.)

## The United States

Following the **highly contentious 1996 elections**, there emerged a tentative political consensus that the United States had **no choice but to remain heavily engaged in maintaining a semblance of "international law and order."** At the same time continued public **concerns about acute U.S. domestic problems** appeared to **weigh heavily against seeking costly military solutions** to the evolving menu of security problems.

In this challenging political context there emerged in 1997 **the Consortium for Planetary Peace (CPP),** an unusual grass roots **political coalition with support from both the left and right** and organized around the twin propositions that: (1) it was **not in the U.S. national interest to become "a global policeman"** and (2) **"modern conflict resolution and communications methods" should be aggressively employed** as flagship elements of U.S. international security policy.

With support from a broad range of existing peace, human-rights, environmental, and other activist groups, the CPP grew quickly with a **"start in your own international neighborhood" organizing theme**--using the Internet to organize a wide range of U.S., Canadian, and Mexican NGOs to **focus a coordinated effort on the continued acute political unrest in southern Mexico.** In late 1998 the organization gained considerable prestige by facilitating a widely hailed "peace agreement" between the Mexican government and the "Third Zapatista Revolution."

Building on the success in Mexico, the CPP over the past year and a half has become **increasingly involved as a mediator and Internet organizer of "peacemaking coalitions" in a number of regional and other conflicts around the world** (in which capacity it has developed substantial informal ties with the Islamic CIRD coalition).

In 1998, an organization was established within the JCS to oversee the **development of offensive and defensive operational concepts and campaigns and new requirements for "electronic warfare techniques."** This organization works with the various unified commands to develop Radio Electronic Combat or IW planning annexes for the CINCs' CONPLANs for various contingencies.

Increasing concerns about the viability of the nuclear non-proliferation regime led in 1998 to **major revisions in U.S. force structure plans to make room for a package of counter-proliferation initiatives** which included: (1) A crash effort on the **Theater High Altitude Air Defense (THAAD)** system, (2) Extensive overseas sales of **Patriot/ERINT** and *Standard* anti-tactical missiles, and (3) Accelerated development of **long-endurance unmanned air vehicles (UAVs)** and a companion program of multi-mission **unattended ground sensors (UGS).**

In late 1999 in the wake of the French AirBus incident reported earlier **U.S. commercial aircraft companies initiated a survey of the software in the flight control systems of aircraft under development** to insure software system integrity. Other than some minor software code errors, nothing was found--but there emerged a heightened vigilance in the commercial aircraft sector to protect these systems.

## Persian Gulf Security

In 1999 in the face of Iran's growing political military power, the **U.S., France, and the U.K. updated their military agreements with the Gulf Coordinating Council (GCC).**

The military contingency plans for the region now include the **prepositioning of substantial additional military equipment in the region** and **rapid deployment commitments** code-named **GREEN HORNET** for the U.S. (see Table 1) and **SILVER SABRE** for the U.K. and France.

A British air mobile/motorized and a French air mobile/motorized division along with several squadrons of tactical fighter aircraft constitute the principal European military components of **SILVER SABRE.**

In 1998, the Joint Staff approved an **IW contingency plan** for CENTCOM combining both **electronic and physical attack: Operation FORCE FIELD**--a **theater-wide command and control warfare master plan** designed to provide "information dominance within a 500 km battle cube" and in particular render ineffective the key elements of a future regional opponent's **tactical** reconnaissance, air defense, and C3I systems.

# SITUATION REPORT (cont.)

Table 1. Major Components of GREEN HORNET

| | Phase One<br>Deterrent Phase | Phase Two<br>Initial Defense | Phase Three<br>Full Capability |
|---|---|---|---|
| Army | • Deploy 2 THAAD battalions<br>• Place 2 Phase Two Divisions on Alert<br>• Deploy Army equipment set from Diego Garcia<br>• Airlift 3 brigades to prepositioned equipment sets in Kuwait and Bahrain | • Fully deploy 2 Phase Two Divisions<br>• Place 4 Phase Three Divisions (3 CONUS/1 Europe) on Alert | • Fully deploy 4 Phase Three Divisions<br>• Reserve call-up |
| Navy | • Move 1 Carrier Battle Group (CBG) to Gulf of Oman<br>• Move 1 *Aegis* to Persian Gulf | • Deploy CBG to Red Sea<br>• Move 1 *Aegis* to Persian Gulf<br>• Move 2 *Aegis* to Med<br>• Partial Ready Reserve Fleet (RRF) call-up | • Deploy 3 CBGs<br>• Move 6 *Aegis* to Theater<br>• Reserve call-up<br>• Full RRF |
| Air Force | • Deploy 1 Air Combat Wing (ACW)<br>• Deploy AWACS, JSTARS, intel aircraft | • Deploy 3 ACWs | • Deploy 7 ACWs |
| Marine Corps | • Deploy 1 Maritime Prepositioning Squadron (MPS) from Diego Garcia and off load in Saudi Arabia<br>• Off load in-Theater MPS<br>• Airlift associated CONUS brigade personnel to theater | • Deploy 2 MPS from Atlantic and Pacific<br>• Marry up 2 CONUS brigades w/in-theater MPS equipment<br>• Deploy 2 amphibious brigades from CONUS | • 2 amphibious brigades in Theater<br>• Reserve call-up |
| Troop Strength | 50,000 | +100,000 = 150,000 | +150,000 = 300,000 |
| Time to Complete (from t=0) | 7 Days | 30 Days | 60 Days |
| CRAF Aircraft Req't | 0 | 120 | 200 |

# SITUATION REPORT (cont.)

## THE CRISIS

### In Caracas

On **May 4, 2000, OPEC ministers met** in Caracas to review production and pricing policy. **Iran, Iraq, Libya, and Algeria were promoting a major cutback in production** with a goal of driving the price to "at least $60 (FY-95 dollars) a barrel."

The Caracas **OPEC meeting ended in total failure** and disarray after three days of tense discussions marked by a final televised **shouting match between the Iranian and Saudi oil ministers.**

### In the Persian Gulf

On May 7 Iran announced that it would soon begin conducting **"military exercises appropriate to the evolving security situation in the Gulf."**

On May 8 the Saudi ruler called in the U.S. Ambassador and expressed **his deep concerns about the Iranians** whom he feared might use the OPEC stalemate as **an excuse for "a move of greatness" in the Gulf.**

On May 10, Tehran radio and television announced that the **Iranian Foreign Minister was flying to Riyadh with an "urgent proposal"** that would "resolve the OPEC stalemate" and "respond to the evolving security situation in the region."

On the evening of May 10, the U.S. Ambassador to Saudi Arabia reported on the contents of the Iranian "proposal:"

• **Iran, Iraq, Saudi Arabia and the other GCC states** should immediately **cut oil production by 20 percent.**

• The **GCC states** should **annul their military agreements with the U.S.** and declare "neutrality" or non-alignment.

• In return Iran would declare the GCC states to be under **"a new Iranian Persian Gulf security umbrella."**

The next day, May 11, U.S. intelligence detected the **preliminary mobilization of three of the six Iranian divisions located near Dezful in southwestern Iran,** including the mobilization of several regiments of heavy equipment transporters designed to rapidly move heavy armor and artillery.

At 2030 local time on May 11, **Saudi Arabia** ordered the **redeployment of one armored division** toward its border with Iraq and a **partial mobilization** of selected reserve elements. Two hours later **Kuwait** placed its army and reserves on a higher level of alert.

### In Egypt

Later that night, **90% of the power in the Cairo area went out for several hours.**

In a message to the Secretary of State the U.S. Ambassador in Cairo noted that there was considerable **uncertainty** about whether the blackout was the product of **"deliberate sabotage or just Egyptian bad luck."**

### In Saudi Arabia

On the evening of May 11 the White House Situation Room received a message from the U.S. ambassador in Riyadh indicating that **the public switched telephone network for Riyadh had suffered a series of massive failures.**

### In Washington

The U.S. National Communications Center reported that, nearly simultaneously with the Saudi disruption, the **base phone system in Fort Lewis, Washington had been subjected to a massive wardialing attack** by personal computers-- apparently initiated by a bulletin board post which stated the dial-in line numbers--which paralyzed phone service for several hours.

On the Saudi problem the CIA had "preliminary indications" that **a hidden "trap door" was used that had apparently been placed into the latest release of code controlling many switching centers of the Saudi PSN.** This code allows **unauthorized passwords** to be used to gain access through **remote maintenance ports.** The source of this problem was unclear although **a radical anti-interventionist group claimed responsibility** on the Internet.

# SITUATION REPORT (cont.)

### In the Persian Gulf Region

At 0500 local time in the Gulf on May 12 (2200 EDT on the 11th), **two Saudi missile gunboats were fired upon by Iranian warships** discovered on an apparent intelligence collection mission off the coast of Al Jubayl.

Twelve Saudi F-15s arrived on the scene in minutes and in the ensuing battle **both of the Saudi gunboats and three Iranian ships were sunk.** Minutes later fifteen Iranian MiG-29s and 31s arrived and in the air battle that followed **nine Iranian aircraft were downed at the cost of five Saudi F-15s.**

At 0630 local time on the 12th, **a S-3B *Viking*** from the CBG *Ronald Reagan* was **fired upon by an Iran missile frigate** while conducting a maritime surveillance mission **over the Straits of Hormuz.**

Thirty minutes later, **F/A-18s and F/A-14s from the *Reagan* found the frigate** some fifteen miles south of Bandar Abbas. The USN aircraft were **confronted by eight Iranian MiG-29s.** During the short air battle **three MiG-29s were shot down and the frigate was sunk** after receiving three *Harpoon* missile hits.

### In Saudi Arabia

At 1100 local time on May 13, **the largest ARAMCO refinery near Dhahran had a catastrophic flow control malfunction** which led to a **large explosion and fire** at a brand new cracking tower.

This event was followed by a **"war communiqué" from a radical Islamic group linked to Iran** asserting that "the enemies of the true faith of Islam were vulnerable to the full range of Islamic might." The statement concluded with the **threat that the economy of the Saudi Kingdom "could be brought to its knees with the touch of a button."**

In a memcon to the Secretary of State, the U.S. Ambassador to Saudi Arabia warned that **the Saudi elite was "horrified by the prospect that Iran might have the capacity to severely disrupt their economy without firing a shot"** and beginning to express **concerns that the United States may be "unable to help the Saudi government respond to this new threat."**

### In Moscow

At a news conference late on May 13 the Russian Foreign Minister called on the **UN Security Council to "immediately seek to mediate a settlement to the escalating crisis"** in the Persian Gulf.

### In Tehran

At 0730 local time on May 14 (0030 EDT) **Iran** sent **messages to the GCC members, the U.S., the U.K., and France** calling for:

- A **cease-fire in place** of all forces on both sides.

- An **immediate freeze on further deployments by "foreign forces"** in the region.

- An **immediate summit at a neutral site** to discuss "a peaceful resolution of a crisis not of Iran's making."

The notes closed by stating that **"if there were not a positive response within 12 hours"** Iran would be **"forced to take actions consistent with its security rights and responsibilities in the Persian Gulf region."**

The notes to the leaders of Kuwait and Saudi Arabia also included a separate and explicit message that Iran would soon **"demonstrate the futility of depending upon the American imperialists for protection from modern weapons systems."**

Early that afternoon local time, **Iran fired three *Nodong I* MRBMs** virtually simultaneously from a field site south of Tehran. Two of the three successfully deployed **previously unseen exoatmospheric penetration aids**.

### In Germany

At 1812 EDT on May 14, the **new high-speed Deutsche Bundesbahn passenger train *Siegfried* traveling at 300 km/hr slammed into an apparently mis-routed freight train** near Frankfurt am Main. German Federal Police estimated that the train wreck had killed over 60 passengers and crew and critically injured another 120 persons.

Within three hours, the CIA issued a preliminary report indicating there was **"clear evidence"** that **the freight train had been misrouted onto the passenger track** with "some evidence" pointing **to a sophisticated intrusion into the Bundesbahn rail control system.**

# SITUATION REPORT (cont.)

### In New York

At a mid-day reception on May 15 sponsored by the CPP, the **Iranian Ambassador** to the UN was overheard to state that **the United States and Western Europe** as "the technologically most advanced powers on the planet" were **highly vulnerable to "21st Century attacks"** by **"states and others who had mastered contemporary computer and telecommunication technology."**

### In Washington

Later on the 15th a preliminary report on the German train crash by the DCI indicated that **a "logic bomb" had been placed into the Deutsche Bundesbahn computer systems, possibly by someone with inside access,** with **"some tenuous evidence pointing to Iran."**

In passing the report to the President that evening the National Security Advisor noted that "NSA had **considerable doubts about the origin of the attack."** Further, he noted **that the CIA's Foreign Terrorism Center was preparing a report voicing the strong suspicion that the tragedy was the product of a conspiracy** which "may or may not be connected with the unfolding events in the Persian Gulf."

### In the United Kingdom

At 1100 GMT on the 16th the Director of Scotland Yard informed the Prime Minister that **the Bank of England had detected "three different sniffer devices of new design in its main funds transfer system"** and that the Bank leadership was very fearful that unauthorized individuals could now enter the funds transfer system, formerly believed to be invulnerable.

### In Atlanta and London

A few hours later CNN and ITN aired **"Special Report" stories** which featured the German train wreck and leaked reports of problems with the Bank of England's funds transfer system. The CNN report stated that **"some Western intelligence agencies" believe that Iran may be employing computer experts from the Russian Mafiya and "renegade software writers" from India** to "threaten the entire economic fabric of the United States and West Europe." The effects of both broadcasts were reinforced by interviews with a wide range of computer security experts.

The **London Stock Exchange Index fell 10% in late trading on the 16th** with investors shifting assets to safer havens.

### In New York

At 1430 EDT on the 16th, **the New York Stock Exchange suffered its largest drop since the crash of 1987.** Even with the tripping of automatic exchange restraints, the Dow had **fallen by nearly 17 percent** by the end of the day's trading. Analysts on CNBC and other business news networks speculated that major **institutional investors were attempting to get out** of the electronically managed market.

At 1500 the oil futures market closed with **the spot oil price at $75 a barrel. Gold prices for the day were up ten percent.**

At 1700 the Security and Exchange Commission(SEC)'s crisis investigating team informed the Secretary of Commerce that **"a pattern of institutional investment manipulation involving as yet unknown parties working through a set of European and Middle Eastern Banks"** had been **"a leading factor in the rapid acceleration in the Dow's mid-afternoon decline."**

### In Germany

That afternoon the **power grid** serving a region of Germany that **included the U.S. Air Base at Rhein Main failed sporadically** when several areas were unexpectedly cut off from the grid. Although power was quickly restored to these areas an assessment of the cause of the failure indicated **intrusion in a key grid information management and control system.**

### In Washington

**At noon EDT on May 17th the Consortium for Planetary Peace (CPP)** announced that an **"emergency mobilization to stop an unnecessary and potentially devastating war"** would take place in the next 48 hours.

# SITUATION REPORT (cont.)

Two hours later the Consortium submitted a formal request to the U.S. Park Police for a permit for the Mall for May 21 for a **"demonstration of support for mediation and opposition to U.S. intervention in Saudi Arabia"** for **"an estimated 100,000 participants."** By nightfall similar permits had been requested in ten other major U.S. cities.

Approval of the Mall and other CPP requests seemed certain and **mobilization of CPP chapters began to** occur through **communiqués sent over the Internet and more traditional media outlets.**

### In the Persian Gulf

Early in the evening on the 18th local time, after receiving reports on **further massing of Iranian armored forces for possible entry into southern Iraq**, increased Iranian naval activity near the Straits of Hormuz, and an Iranian "strategic alert," **USCINCCENT** sent a **message recommending the immediate execution of Phases I and II of the GREEN HORNET Gulf deployment plan.**

### In Delaware

At 1440 the **PSN for Delaware and Maryland's Eastern Shore** began to suffer a **series of failures** in the face of what appeared to be repeated attacks of unknown origin. The attacks focused on a set of **communications switches** whose failure in all cases **brought down the air traffic control facility at Dover Air Force Base.**

### In Washington

An **emergency NSC meeting** was convened at 1500 EDT on the 18th to address USCINCCENT's recommendation and other military, diplomatic, and political issues related to the evolving Gulf crisis.

The meeting opened with an intelligence briefing by **the DCI** who emphasized the uncertainty in the source or sources of the attack and noted that at this time there was **"no way of knowing for sure"** whether what we are seeing is:

**(1) Testing of strategic IW capability by one or more parties,**

**(2) The beginning of a dedicated IW campaign to derail anticipated U.S. Gulf deployment plans, or**

**(3) Most of what we can expect from a strategic IW campaign mounted by Iran or others."**

He also emphasized the added complication that **anti-interventionist international political groups** in both the U.S. and Europe **could be behind many of the IW incidents.**

The CJCS Chairman immediately emphasized that the **Time Phased Force Deployment List (TPFDL) for GREEN HORNET** was very dependent on the ability to meet "a host of just-in-time logistic timelines" and **would not tolerate "any significant disruption."**

He also expressed growing concern about the **problem of mobilizing the CRAF aircraft and crews** that were "key to Phase II of GREEN HORNET" **if someone were able to penetrate the management information systems of major U.S. airlines.**

In the highly speculative discussion that immediately followed it became very clear that in spite of "circumstantial evidence" pointing to Iran **there remained considerable uncertainty about the extent of Iranian involvement in the recent IW incidents.**

The discussion eventually turned to the military situation in the Gulf where after further reviewing the military and diplomatic issues on the table, the **President** announced the following **decisions:**

- Execute **Phases I and II of GREEN HORNET.**

- Deploy one-half all available CONUS-based **ATBM battalions to Egypt and Saudi Arabia.**

- Set up a **trilateral video conference** with the British Prime Minister and the President of France to gain agreement of these governments to **execute SILVER SABRE.**

- Immediately convene the **North Atlantic Council.**

- **Reject** any **diplomatic initiatives** at this time with **Iran or the CIRD.**

# SITUATION REPORT (cont.)

The President also indicated that he wanted to **obtain Congressional approval of his actions** through a resolution to be introduced in the Congress on the 19th.

The President then led a further in-depth discussion of the IW situation in which he expressed particular concerns about the **long- and short-term implications** of possible successful **IW attacks against U.S. and allied Persian Gulf deployment plans** and the **national information infrastructures of the U.S. and its European allies and key coalition partners in the Gulf region.** He emphasized the need to **"demonstrate persuasively and as soon as possible"** that further IW attacks such as those already experienced would **not be able to fundamentally undermine U.S. military strategy** in the current crisis.

During the discussion the President strongly admonished the Press Secretary to **"keep the lid on"** and **"downplay all speculation"** regarding both **the extent of U.S. cyberspace vulnerabilities** and **the origins of the IW attacks** experienced to date especially those in the U.S. He noted that **further decisions** on the crisis **could be made even more difficult** if there were public panic growing out of **"media hyping" of the IW threat to the U.S.** and **attributing the attacks to date to Iran** when **the actual source might be "domestic anti-interventionist political forces."**

In closing the meeting the President turned to the SECDEF and asked him to see if **he could pull together some information security experts to generate "new or creative ideas" that could be brought to bear "in the near term"** on the IW problems of principal concern in the crisis.

Another NSC meeting was scheduled for late the next morning to review the results of the trilateral discussions and again address the IW problem.

Upon leaving the meeting, the SECDEF **contacted the Director of ARPA** and instructed him to immediately **assemble a tiger team of information system security experts** to address the IW-related issues and concerns that had come up at the NSC meeting. The SECDEF described the President's principal concerns and asked for recommendations on **possible "near-term creative solutions" to the problems** posed "beyond the standard procedures to tighten

information systems security that the services and the CINCs would be likely to take on their own."

### In Washington, London, and Paris

At 1630 EDT on the 18th at a **trilateral video conference** between the President, the British Prime Minister, and the President of France it was agreed that the U.K. and France would join in the U.S. response to the crisis and **execute SILVER SABRE.** It was also agreed that the three countries should keep each other **fully informed of further developments in terms of possible IW attacks.**

# STEP ONE: The Day Of...

# INSTRUCTIONS

## How to Proceed

1. You have been selected as a **member of a technical tiger team** advising **the Secretary of Defense** and the Director of ARPA, in a **time-urgent process**. The group's task is to revise a draft memo to the SECDEF in preparation for the ARPA Director's meeting with the SECDEF scheduled for a few hours hence.

2. The group's tasking is to produce an assessment for the SECDEF to send to the President proposing **possible short-term technical solutions** to these pressing cyberspace problems.

## The Chair(person)

1. The tiger team will be led in its deliberations by a Chairperson (hereinafter Chair) who will take the group through the tasking described in the **Decisions to Be Made** section to the right.

2. The Chair will ask one participant to record the results of the group's deliberations and recommendations.

3. The Chair will likely begin by asking for participants in her/his group to <u>very briefly</u> (e.g., in a few sentences) give their **individual perspectives** on the overall situation and the particular challenge presented to the group.

## Decisions to Be Made

### I. Issues and Options

An ARPA staff working group has prepared an incomplete **Draft Memo for the President** on the following pages. It essentially provides a **working template** of what might go forward on a set of emergency technical and procedural "information assurance" issues related to the current crisis.

Under the guidance of the Chair, the group should discuss and expand this Draft Memo as judged appropriate. In particular the Chair should ascertain whether there are **other critical issues beyond those presented** which the SECDEF might bring up at this point in time--and modify the Draft Memo accordingly.

It should be kept in mind that the group is not being convened primarily as a decision-making body; **the group's principal responsibility is to craft a good issues and options memo** to send forward to the President.

### 2. Recommendations

As the group settles on the individual issues and options to go forward to the SECDEF, the Chair should attempt to see **if consensus can be reached on recommendations** on individual issues--keeping in mind that at this point a consensus on all issues is not expected.

When the time for STEP ONE is up, the Chair of each group will be asked to **summarized very concisely** the group's deliberations and recommendations. This summary should be brief-- if at all possible, **not more than five minutes.**

# STEP ONE: The Day Of...

# Draft Memo for the Secretary of Defense

---

## DEPARTMENT OF DEFENSE

19 May 2000

MEMORANDUM FOR:     President

FROM:     Secretary of Defense

SUBJECT:     Tiger Team Recommendations on Persian Gulf Crisis - Information Warfare Issues

In response to your request at the May 18 NSC meeting, we proceeded to assemble an ARPA-led "tiger team" of information security experts to consider the information warfare (IW) aspects of the ongoing Persian Gulf crisis and make recommendations on:

• Near-term measures to strengthen as quickly as possible the U.S. Defense Information Infrastructure (DII) and other U.S. and allied/coalition information systems critical to the GREEN HORNET and SILVER SABRE deployment plans and our overall military strategy in this crisis, and

• Other possible measures to strengthen the national information infrastructure (NII) of the U.S. and the NIIs of our allies and coalition partners against possible strategic IW attacks.

PRINCIPAL IW-RELATED OBJECTIVES

Consistent with your public statement and guidance at previous NSC meetings, my guidance to the team was that our principal long-term objectives in this situation in terms of IW are:

• Demonstrate broad U.S. capability to detect, assess, and effectively defend against IW attacks targeted on critical U.S. defense and national information systems.

• Foster the development of cooperative efforts with U.S. allies and coalition partners that achieve comparable capabilities in response to IW attacks against their key information systems.

• Deter future strategic IW attacks of the kind that we appear to be experiencing in the current crisis.

I also told them that your principal <u>short-term</u> objectives in terms of IW are:

- Ensure that the GREEN HORNET and SILVER SABRE deployment plans proceed without serious disruption due to IW attacks.

- Identify the source(s) of the recent series of IW-related events.

- Take concrete defensive IW actions which can be made public and serve to reassure the American public that we can respond effectively to cyberspace attacks against the DII and key U.S. NII systems.

- Assist Saudi Arabia in responding to the IW attacks on its NII in order to enhance the prospects that the Saudi government will survive the threat posed by the internal dissident movement and Iran.

## ORGANIZATION OF THIS MEMORANDUM

In response to the tasking summarized above, below you will find a set of recommended near-term actions for your consideration along with preliminary assessment of possible implementation obstacles.  The issues and recommendations have been organized as follows:

I. Issues Related to GREEN HORNET/SILVER SABRE
  A. DII Issues
  B. Other Related U.S. NII Issues
  C. Allied/Coalition Partner Information Systems Issues

II. Issues Related to IW Tactical Warning/Attack Assessment

III. Issues Related to Strategic IW Attacks on the U.S. NII

IV. Issues Related to Strategic IW Attacks on Allies and Coalition Partners

## I. ISSUES RELATED TO GREEN HORNET/SILVER SABRE

You expressed particular concern about the tight timelines for both the GREEN HORNET and SILVER SABRE deployment plans and the possible vulnerability of these plans to disruption by IW attack by either the Iranians, the CIRD, or domestic political forces opposed to Western intervention in the Gulf crisis.

As you are aware from earlier assessments, we do not at this point know the full extent of the capacity of any of these entities to disrupt a U.S. deployment to the Gulf. We have already seen one kind of attack--the mass dialing attack on the base phone system at Ft. Lewis, WA--that could potentially cause problems if widespread (i.e., if it occurred at a large number of U.S. military bases involved in GREEN HORNET) and sustained for many days.

In examining the different elements of the GREEN HORNET and SILVER SABRE deployment plans we see potentially serious IW-related problems in the following areas:

• Sustained IW attacks that disrupt and degrade U.S. and European air traffic control systems (ATCS).

• Sustained IW attacks on the information systems of U.S. airlines that are supplying Civilian Reserve Aircraft Fleet (CRAF) aircraft and crews to support GREEN HORNET.

• IW attacks that succeed in modifying the Time Phased Force Deployment List (TPFDL) for GREEN HORNET.

• IW attacks on the PSN in the U.S., Britain, and France.

•

•

•

•

•

As you know, under current planning we do not need to communicate large amounts of information to support the initial "Deterrent Phase" deployments for GREEN HORNET (beyond the "Go" message which has already been passed to the relevant military units). Nevertheless we need to be concerned about disruption of the air traffic control system here and in Europe since the efficient operation of these ATC systems is key to maintaining the fast pace of these initial deployments.

The second "Initial Defense" phase is more complex and potentially more vulnerable to disruption both here in the United States (since it involves CRAF aircraft and far more extensive rail and air transport of troops and equipment) and in Europe (since it involves U.S. forces stationed in Europe and the British and French SILVER SABRE forces). The same is true of the third deployment phase which is necessary to achieve full offensive and defensive capability in the Gulf region. The amount of communications involved (relating to logistics and transportation and other logistics matters) is also much greater in both of these phases than in the initial deployment phase which raises more serious PSN concerns.

The recommendations of the tiger team in terms of possible near-term technical responses to these GREEN HORNET/SILVER SABRE IW-related problems (and possible implementation obstacles) are as follows:

| A. DII Issues | |
|---|---|
| Recommended Technical Response | Possible Implementation Obstacles |

| | |
|---|---|
| 1. Close all possible firewalls to and within DII systems | • |
| 2. Disable all remote dial-in maintenance ports on DII system telecommunications switches | • Alternative maintenance procedures may prove inefficient and lead to selected system failures or delays |
| 3. Provide 24-hr. system operator monitoring and overview of all critical information system nodes with special attention paid to detecting disruptions and abnormal system behavior | • |
| 4. | • |
| 5. | • |

| B. Other Related U.S. NII Issues | |
|---|---|
| Recommended Technical Response | Possible Implementation Obstacles |
| 1. <u>(re PSN)</u> Route all critical GREEN HORNET Phase Two/Three communications over available robust command and control channels rather than relying on the U.S. PSN | • Could result in significant delays in GREEN HORNET Phase Two/Three communications and thus in deployment timelines |
| 2. <u>(re ATCS)</u> | • |
| 3.<u>(re CRAF)</u> | • Need to ensure security of commercial airlines' main scheduling system |
| 4. <u>(re Power Grid)</u> | • |

| C. Allied/Coalition Partner Information Systems Issues | |
|---|---|
| Recommended Technical Response | Possible Implementation Obstacles |
| 1. <u>(re European PSN's)</u> | • |
| 2. <u>(re European ATCS's)</u> | • |
| 3. | • |

## II. ISSUES RELATED TO IW TACTICAL WARNING/ATTACK ASSESSMENT (TW/AA)

You have indicated that among your main concerns was an inability to identify the source(s) of the various IW attacks that have recently taken place and the total absence of any warning relating to these attacks. This has given rise to related uncertainties as to whether the attacks represented Iranian (or other potential sources) testing of their IW capability, the beginnings of a much larger IW campaign, or most of what we might have to deal with in terms of strategic IW attacks during the current crisis.

The tiger team judged that the tactical warning/attack assessment (TW/AA) problem to be extremely difficult. In approaching this issue, they concluded that existing legal constraints or impediments to this problem might be removed in crisis in order to have any hope of improving the TW/AA situation.

The recommendations of the ARPA tiger team in terms of possible near-term technical responses to these tactical warning/attack assessment (TW/AA) IW-related problems are as follows:

| TW/AA Issues | |
|---|---|
| Recommended Technical Response | Possible Implementation Obstacles |
| 1. (re Tactical Warning)<br>  • Place automated software "backtrack" programs in those information systems that have already been subject to attack and at other likely targets | • Legal challenges |
|   • Begin emergency development of a tactical warning and attack assessment scheme based on the follow design philosophy and system components:<br>    ••<br><br>    ••<br><br><br>  • | • |
| 2. (re Attack Assessment)<br>  • | • |

## III. ISSUES RELATED TO STRATEGIC IW ATTACKS ON THE U.S. NII

You expressed particular concern about the domestic political impact, and thus the broad political-military impact in the crisis, of successful strategic IW attacks against key elements of the U.S. NII--and the resultant loss of the national sanctuary that the American people have enjoyed for nearly two centuries.

With this perspective in mind, the tiger team looked at possible near-term measures to enhance the security of the key elements of the U.S. NII relating to: (1) the PSN, (2) the transportation system, (3) the electric power grid, and (4) the oil and gas pipeline system.

The recommendations of the team in terms of possible near-term technical responses to possible strategic IW attacks on the U.S. NII are as follows:

| U.S. NII Strategic IW Attack Issues | |
|---|---|
| Recommended Technical Response | Possible Implementation Obstacles |
| 1. (re the PSN) <br> • | • |
| 2. (re Transportation Systems) <br> • | • |
| 4. (re the Electric Power Grid) <br> • | • |
| 5. (re the Oil And Gas Pipeline System <br> • | • |

## IV. ISSUES RELATED TO STRATEGIC IW ATTACKS ON ALLIES AND COALITION PARTNERS

Our European allies and regional coalition partners Saudi Arabia and Egypt appear already to be in the throes of some kind of strategic IW campaign designed to weaken their resolve in the crisis.

The approach that the tiger team took to this problem was as follows:

> • Look for technical solutions to the vulnerability of the Saudi PSN sufficient to insure that the Saudi government could maintain a limited but high-confidence communications network for the country as a whole.

55

- For other elements of the Saudi NII and the Egyptian and European NII's look for general technical solutions to enhance the survivability and overall viability of key information systems.

With this approach the recommendations of the tiger team in terms of possible near-term technical responses to possible strategic IW attacks on the NII's of U.S. European allies and coalition partners are as follows:

| Allies/Coalition Partners NII Strategic IW Attack Issues | |
|---|---|
| Recommended Technical Response | Possible Implementation Obstacles |
| 1. (re the Saudi PSN)<br>• Make emergency modifications to U.S. dedicated secure communications equipment so that it can be given to the Saudis now, but selectively disabled at a later time of our choosing.<br><br>• Assist the Saudis in fencing off selected PSN circuits. | •<br><br>• |
| 2. (re other NII Systems of European Allies and Coalition Partners)<br>• Send a crack team of computer security specialists to work collectively with our allies on all key software system and application code controlling major rail, pipeline, telecommunications, and power grid systems.<br><br>• Offer use of U.S. "server" computer systems containing substantial firewall software to help isolate key European information system connections through which IW attacks may be launched.<br><br>• | •<br><br>•<br><br>• |

# STEP ONE (cont.) -- Recent Developments

## SITUATION REPORT

### THE CONTINUING CRISIS

The following is a synopsis of developments in the crisis since the initial report you were given.

### MAY 20

**In the United States**

On the morning of May 20th the **U.S. Senate passed a resolution supporting the President's decision to send troops to the Gulf.** The margin of victory for the Administration was **two votes.**

That morning **the automatic tellers of the largest bank chain in Georgia malfunctioned** with bank clients being debited and/or credited thousands of the dollars after each ATM transaction--leading the bank to **shut down its ATM network.** Bank officials stated that it must have been **"an inside job"** since they had recently installed a new release of the ATM software about three weeks ago and suspected a logic bomb triggered by some means.

Early that afternoon the **CNN news center feed out of Atlanta was intermittently off the air for twelve minutes.**

On May 20 DoD discovered that **the computer data base for the Time Phased Force Deployment List (TPFDL) had become plagued with "corrupt data."** The JCS IW planning cell's initial report on the problem indicated that **a computer worm--origin uncertain--had likely been unleashed inside the TPFDL software** through a **personal computer temporarily linked to the TPFDL** system running popular commercial off-the-shelf database software with a known security flaw.

### MAY 21

**In the United States**

On the morning of May 21 the U.S. Ambassador in Egypt notified the Secretary of State that the President of Egypt had become **"very concerned about Iran's capacity to cause economic and political damage in Egypt."**

That morning the Pentagon first revealed their concerns about **delays in military deployments to the Gulf** due to **IW attacks** on the **local area networks and phone systems** of a number of **key Army and Marine bases.**

Early in the afternoon of May 21 **a new Continental Airlines AB-340** making a final instrumented approach to **O'Hare International Airport suffered a massive malfunction** in its **flight deck avionics** and minutes later **crashed in a residential area** killing **all 236 passengers and crew** and 36 **people on the ground.**

Later that day the FAA **grounded all late model AB-340 and 330 aircraft** on the basis that **the flight control software might be infected by a sophisticated logic bomb.**

That evening the **Justice Department** reported the interrogation of **two suspects at a San Antonio, Texas software firm** which had provided the **most recent update of the AB-340 flight control software.** (Both had recently received large cash payments through a Swiss bank.) Although the **source code for the flight control software had been checked line-by-line** before installation, the two suspects apparently had **access to the compiler,** and presumably modified it to cause unauthorized actions in the compiled control software.

The May 21 CPP **"anti-intervention" demonstration in Washington** drew **a crowd estimated by the U.S. Park Police at over 400,000.** Many other well-attended demonstrations in both large and small cities across the country were also organized via the Internet.

# SITUATION REPORT (cont.)

## MAY 22

### In the United States

At an NSC Meeting early on the morning of May 22 **the President was briefed on:**

   (1) **Operation IRON LANCE - an all-out preemptive air and missile strike against Iranian conventional forces threatening Saudi Arabia** and

   (2) **Operation FORCE FIELD - a theater-wide command and control attack plan.**

A **highly contentious debate** on both operations followed but **no decisions were taken** on either operation.

### In Saudi Arabia

At 1920 local time (1220 EDT) on May 22, the news anchors of the two Saudi government TV networks were **suddenly replaced by the face of the head of the CIRD Council** who called on the citizens of Saudi Arabia to **overthrow the monarchy. Large scale demonstrations** against the Saudi monarchy began shortly thereafter **in Riyadh, Jiddah, Mecca, and Dhahran.**

That same day **the Saudi public switched network began to fail again.** The failure was attributed to unauthorized modification of the system through **trap doors in the logic controlling its switches - which were very similar to those found earlier in the failure of the Saudi PSN."** (The Saudi telecom system was **purchased from the same company** supplying approximately 30% of the U.S. PSN.)

By that evening the self-described **"Provisional Islamic Republic of Arabia"** had **seized power in Dhahran and Mecca.**

That evening saw the beginning of **heavy fighting in Riyadh** between **security police** and **members of the National Guard** which had pledged their loyalty to the new Provisional Islamic Republic. Within hours the U.S. Ambassador reported that fighting was spreading rapidly throughout the city and that **a coup attempt** was underway.

## MAY 23

### In the United States

On the morning of May 23 the CJCS reported to the SECDEF a **"full-scale IW attack"** by **unknown sources against almost every U.S. military base involved in GREEN HORNET and SILVER SABRE.** His report also stated bluntly that **the TPFDL was "a goddamned mess"** and that he had **"no idea"** what kind of **GREEN HORNET schedule was achievable."**

At a mid-morning Atlanta news conference the members of the "Executive Council" of the **Consortium for Planetary Peace announcing** that the CPP was **"mobilizing all of its chapters to conduct civil disobedience actions** to stop the U.S. Government's mad dash to war to save an undemocratic and failed Saudi regime."

At 1230 EDT on the 23rd **the Chicago Commodity Exchange** experienced its **wildest fluctuations in history** and **halted trading** on the grounds that the Exchange was apparently being **subjected to a powerful form of electronic manipulation** by unknown parties.

In mid-afternoon the **entire phone network in the Washington/Baltimore region including local cellular systems failed.** The attack was **attributed to trap doors** not unlike those that caused the earlier PSN failure in Saudi Arabia. Preliminary indications were that **only 70% of the switches were disabled**, but that remaining carriers and switches could not handle the additional load.

At 1700 EDT the President asked the National Security Advisor to arrange an NSC Meeting for the next morning so he could **"assess the overall situation and especially our defensive IW prospects"** in order to decide on **"next steps"** in the crisis.

It is now 1900 on May 23, 2000.

# STEP TWO: The Day Before...

# INSTRUCTIONS

### How to Proceed

1. You will have a total of two hours for STEP TWO --roughly 10 minutes for reading and the remainder of the two hours for deliberations.

2. The time period is the very near future--say the late spring of 1996.

3. You are again in the role of a top advisor to the Director of ARPA, preparing him for a meeting with the Secretary of Defense on a national R&D investment strategy for information systems security and related issues.

4. The Chair will lead a discussion that moves through the tasking described in the Decisions to Be Made section to the right--which follows essentially the same basic process as the previous two steps.

### Decisions to Be Made

#### I. Issues and Options

The objective of the meeting with the SECDEF that the Director of ARPA will attend is to formulate both U.S. and Defense research strategies addressing a set of near-term issues that have emerged from a study commissioned by a Presidential Review Directive on: (1) threats to national security and safety arising from the evolution of new information warfare (IW) techniques and (2) means that can be used to help counter those threats.

The staff-prepared Draft Memo for the Secretary of Defense (on the pages immediately following) is designed to serve this purpose.

Under the guidance of the Chair, the group should discuss this Draft Memo and expand and modify it as judged appropriate.

#### 2. Recommendations

When the group settles on the material to go forward to the SECDEF, it should attempt under the Chair's leadership to **see if it can reach consensus** on a recommendation on the issues in the Draft Memo--keeping in mind that **consensus is not necessarily expected;** the SECDEF invariably will have to make some decisions.

When it is clear to the Chair that there is a division of views on an issue, vote on the options still on the table and record the vote.

# STEP TWO: The Day Before...

# Draft Memo for the Secretary of Defense

**Advanced Research Projects Agency**

xx XXXXXX 1996

MEMORANDUM FOR:     The Secretary of Defense

FROM:     Director, Advanced Research Projects Agency

SUBJECT:     A Research Strategy Addressing Threats to National Security and Safety from New Techniques of Information Warfare

This memorandum presents discussion issues for the meeting tomorrow on a new R&D investment strategy for DoD and the nation as a whole to respond to threats to national security and safety arising from the evolution of new information warfare (IW) techniques.

The recently completed interagency study on this subject emphasized that our national interests are increasingly dependent on a set of information systems critical not only to U.S. military operations but also more broadly to U.S. health, safety, and commerce. A range of critical U.S. information systems appear to be vulnerable to a spectrum of possible IW attacks, including disruption and denial of service, implanting false data, covert installation of harmful programs (e.g., viruses), and the outright theft of information. Unlike other threats to U.S. national security, the "cost of entry" to potential attackers is extremely low, enabling attacks to be initiated by a wide range of sources including other nations, "hackers," terrorists, zealots, disgruntled insiders, criminals, and commercial organizations.

Because of the unconventional nature of this new strategic threat, it is increasingly clear that traditional R&D approaches are not fully appropriate to assessing risks and devising counters to specific threats.

Another problem is that "cyberspace" transcends our national borders and has traditionally been a forum exhibiting and facilitating freedom of interconnection and expression. There are no current regulations or licensing provisions governing who can connect to the Internet, much less government-mandated systems and security provisions. This raises questions as to how aggressive the U.S. can or should be in pursuing the imposition of restrictions or technical solutions on cyberspace.

The set of research approaches set forth below attempt to give structure and clarity to several key facets of this complex problem that would appear to warrant <u>near-term</u> attention.

# 1. INVESTMENT STRATEGY

In the items below we have identified several key issues that relate explicitly to the overall question of investment strategy.

## 1.1 Commercial Software

Although substantial security techniques and devices have been developed, by and large they are not incorporated in the widely used commercially available operating systems and programs (e.g., Windows 95; commercial UNIX systems). To be effective, existing technology and procedures should become widespread.

What steps should the U.S. and DoD take to ensure that known security technology becomes embedded in widely-available commercial operating systems and applications?

_____ A. Assure that key developers of commercial software are part of the development process for new security technology;

_____ B. _____

_____

_____ C. _____

_____

**The ARPA recommendation is that we pursue Option** _____.

**Possible implementation obstacles for this option:** _____

_____

In addition (on the matter of commercial software issues) ARPA recommends:

_____

_____

_____

_____

_____

_____

## 1.2 <u>Minimum Essential Information Infrastructure</u>

Broad benefits have been derived from the open information architecture and information-sharing that has to date characterized the evolution of the NII and the GII. Retaining these benefits, while meeting the critical needs of cyberspace safety and security, poses a major challenge.

In this context a key issue for near-term decision is whether to launch an effort to establish a Minimum Essential Information Infrastructure (MEII) to meet a variety of national security emergency preparedness needs--for example, ensuring that regional force deployments that depend heavily on the operations of segments of the NII are resilient to attack. Such an MEII would be analogous to the Minimum Essential Emergency Communications Network (MEECN) that was designed to insure the execution of U.S. nuclear war plans.

There are, however, serious questions as to whether key NII infrastructure components are too interdependent to isolate a manageable subset as "minimum essential." One approach to this problem might be to select the parts of the NII most critical to military and civilian operations and then defending them by whatever means appropriate and affordable. As an example, a portion of the infrastructure might be placed on dedicated fiber optic cables with protected input/output switches procured by the Defense Department to ensure essential point-to-point communications to enhance force deployment capabilities. In addition, modifications to existing laws might allow cooperation between the intelligence community and domestic law enforcement agencies to improve the gathering of intelligence on U.S. citizens who operate in cyberspace performing actions counter to U.S. national interests--or imposes some protection standards. Another component might be a tax incentive to encourage commercial firms to cooperate with U.S government-led protection processes and encourage development of rapid reconstitution capabilities.

The most promising strategy for the U.S. to pursue in developing an MEII would be:

      _____ A. Select some subset of existing telecommunications links to be hardened or specially protected in some manner.

      _____ B. Create a separate secure U.S. backbone telecommunication structure to which critical communications may be diverted in an emergency.

      _____ C. _____

      _____

      _____ D _____

      _____

**The ARPA recommendation is that we pursue Option** _____.

    **Possible implementation obstacles for this option:** _____

_____

In addition (on the matter of an MEII) ARPA recommends:

_____

_____

_____

_____

_____

_____

1.3 <u>(Subject)</u> _____

_____

_____

_____ A. _____

_____

_____ B. _____

_____

_____ C. _____

_____

## 2. NEW OPERATIONAL CONCEPTS AND PRACTICES

### 2.1 Tactical Warning and Attack Assessment (TW/AA)

Information and telecommunications systems--and systems dependent on them--
sometimes fail, either catastrophically (e.g., the "Northeast blackout") or more
narrowly (one major carrier's long-distance lines were once unavailable for 6
hours). Earthquakes, hurricanes, tornadoes, and other natural phenomena
cause disruptions. Given normal exigencies, it may well be difficult to tell
whether the U.S. is being subjected to a coordinated IW attack. We should have
warning regarding whether we are under attack, and if so by whom.

The following are some possible approaches to TW/AA.

_____ A. For critical national information systems, mandate the
generation of unassailable audit trails recording transactions passing
through key nodes, supplemented by "expert systems" or other agent-
type software continuously monitoring for unusual patterns.
Automatically report unusual data to a central "clearing house" node for
higher-level pattern analysis and interpretation.

_____ B. Significantly expand the concept of CERTs (Computer
Emergency Response Teams) to cover all key national information
systems. These provide human analysis and interpretation of events as
they are reported by automated information-gathering nodes and
reporting by systems administrators.

_____ C. _____

_____

_____ D _____

_____

**The ARPA recommendation is that we pursue Option** _____.

**Possible implementation obstacles for this option:** _____

_____

### 2.2 People and Procedures as the Weak Link in Security

Substantial research and development programs in computer and network
security have been undertaken--by ARPA and others--over the past 20 years,
yet the vast majority of computers and networks in use within the U.S. and its
information infrastructure are insecure. Reasons for this include: (1) inertia;
(2) lack of perception of a problem--benefits do not appear to outweigh costs for
any individual site or organization; (3) no central point of control; (4) lax
operational procedures, including physical security.

64

If we are to have greater information assurance in our systems, in addition to addressing technical solutions these "people and procedures" aspects of the problem must also be addressed as well as technical solutions:

_____ A. Substantially greater programs in education and training of system operators and users;

_____ B. "Make 'em feel it."  Develop, support and encourage "red-teams" to attack key portions of our national information infrastructure to demonstrate security flaws in systems and operational procedures, with ensuing embarrassment and possible sanctions for those found inadequate;

_____ C. _____

_____

_____ D _____

_____

**The ARPA recommendation is that we pursue Option** _____.

**Possible implementation obstacles for this option:** _____

_____

In addition (on the matter of people and procedures issues) ARPA recommends:

_____

_____

2.3. <u>(Subject)</u> _____

_____

_____

_____ A. _____

_____

_____ B. _____

_____

_____ C. _____

_____

## 3. R&D PROGRAM

In the items below we have identified several possible new R&D initiatives (or new R&D priorities) to enhance information systems security.

### 3.1 Trusted Insiders

Trusted insiders are a particular security problem. For less than the cost of a major, targeted computer and network hacking/cracking campaign, it may often be possible to "buy" the services of a disgruntled trusted insider who already possesses the needed passwords, physical access codes, and knowledge of operating procedures.

The basic options for countering this weakness in many infrastructure information systems are:

_____ A. Work toward creating systems that are autonomous and require many fewer "insiders" for their operation;

_____ B. Research on "tamper-proof" audit trails and system monitoring devices that cannot be bypassed or defeated by an insider, and will provide warning and evidence of any wrongdoing;

_____ C. _____

_____.

_____ D. _____

_____.

**The ARPA recommendation is that we pursue Option** _____.

**Possible implementation obstacles for this option:** _____

_____

In addition (on the matter of trusted insiders) ARPA recommends:

_____

_____

### 3.2 New Security Techniques

Existing information security techniques (firewalls, encapsulation, multi-level secure operating systems, passwords, etc.) are not widely and effectively employed throughout the key national information systems or in mass-market commercial operating systems and networks, and they are viewed as difficult to use. (The two factors are of course not unrelated.)

There may be fundamentally new techniques upon which the U.S. might base the security of its information infrastructure. Possible examples might include: (1) a "biological immune system" metaphor (currently being explored by some scientists) in which systems have both "barrier" (e.g., skin, cell membrane) defenses and "active" defenses (e.g., generating antibodies tailored to antigens); (2) Detection and rapid recovery; bad things--foreseen and unforeseen--will happen to information systems, rather than protecting against all foreseen dangers, concentrate on designing systems that recover fast enough that ill effects from their downtime or disablement are not severe.

The possible new techniques that the U.S. might explore in pursuit of a breakthrough in national information infrastructure security are:

_____ A. _____

_____

_____.

_____ B. _____

_____

_____.

**The ARPA recommendation is that we pursue Option** _____.

**Possible implementation obstacles for this option**: _____

_____

In addition (on the matter of new security techniques ) ARPA recommends:

_____

_____

3.3 <u>(Subject)</u> _____

_____

_____

_____ A. _____

_____

_____ B. _____

_____

# References

Anderson, D., T. Fribold, and A. Valdes (1995). *Next Generation Intrusion Detection Expert System (NIDES): A Summary*, SRI-CSL-95-07. Menlo Park, CA: SRI International.

Anderson, D., T. F. Lunt, H. Javitz, A. Tamaru, and A. Valdes (1995). *Detecting Unusual Program Behavior Using the Statistical Component of the Next Generation Intrusion Detection Expert System (NIDES)*, SRI-CSL-95-06. Menlo Park, CA: SRI International.

Forrest, S., A. S. Perelson, L. Allen, and R. Cherukuri (1994). "Self-nonself discrimination in a computer," in *Proc. 1994 IEEE Symposium on Research in Security and Privacy*.

Hundley, R., and R. Anderson (1995). "Emerging Challenge: Security and Safety in Cyberspace," *IEEE Technology and Society Magazine*, Vol. 14, No. 4, Winter 1995-1996, pp. 19-28. Reprinted in RAND RP-484.

Kephart, J. O. (1994). "A Biologically Inspired Immune System for Computers," in R. A. Brooks and P. Maes (eds.), *Artificial Life IV, Proceedings of the Fourth International Workshop on Synthesis and Simulation of Living Systems*. Cambridge, MA: MIT Press, pp. 130-139.

Mesic, R., R. Molander, and P. Wilson (1995). *Strategic Futures: Evolving Missions for Traditional Strategic Delivery Vehicles*, RAND, MR-375-DAG.

Millot, D., R. Molander, and P. Wilson (1993). *The Day After... Study: Nuclear Proliferation in the Post-Cold War World*, Vols. I–III. RAND, MR-266-AF, MR-253-AF, MR-267-AF.

Molander, R., A. Riddile, and P. Wilson (1995). "Nuclear Command, Control, Communications and Intelligence Review Adjunct," RAND, internal paper.

Molander, R., A. Riddile, and P. Wilson (1996). *Strategic Information Warfare: A New Face of War*, RAND, MR-661-OSD.

Molander, R., P. Wilson, R. Mesic, and S. Gardiner (1994). *Under the Nuclear Shadow: Power Projection in the Post-Cold War World*, RAND, MR-513-AF.

Venema, W. (1992). "TCP Wrapper: Network Monitoring, Access Control, and Booby Traps," in *Proceedings of the 3rd Unix Security Symposium*, Baltimore, MD, September 1992. Also available via Web site ftp://ftp.win.tue.nl/pub/security/index.html.